YELLOW BALLOONS

Finding Power to Live above Your Circumstances

by

TIM DUNN

D0062372

EQUIP PRESS
Colorado Springs, Colorado

YELLOW BALLOONS

Finding Power to Live above Your Circumstances

First Edition: 2018
Yellow Balloons / Tim Dunn
Paperback ISBN: 978-1-946453-29-7
eBook ISBN: 978-1-946453-30-3

ENDORSEMENTS

"Some rare people are so bright and get so much done I think of them as extraordinary. I usually also think they should write a book so the rest of us could get some idea how they do all they do. My friend Tim Dunn is one of those rare extraordinary people, but he is even rarer in that he has indeed written a book! I hope you will take advantage of that and read it and apply its wisdom in your own life."

Eric Metaxas
NY Times bestselling author of *Martin Luther* and *If You Can Keep It*

"This is a practical book. Gritty like the Texas town Tim Dunn grew up in. Direct yet endearing. Compact yet profound. Themes like faith, testing, and empowerment come alive in unique ways, all designed to help us shape a vital, godly perspective. Don't miss the richness that comes from Dunn's down-to-earth style. I read every word and wanted more."

John D. Beckett
Chairman, The Beckett Companies; Board member, Cru International; author of *Loving Monday* and *Mastering Monday*

"After a year of trying to get pregnant, I suffered a miscarriage. It was devastating for both me and my husband. Having finished Yellow Balloons *just weeks beforehand, I had a fresh perspective for life in the valley. My trust in God during the storm was transformed. Tim's vulnerability and struggle in discovering God's truths about living through life's varied terrains is a journey we all need to take. As a leadership coach, I regularly share the wisdom gleaned from these pages in hopes of encouraging and empowering others into greater freedom and ownership. As a woman, wife, and fellow traveler, I cannot recommend this book enough."*

Kylie Willis
Leadership Coach

"Drawing from the pages of Scripture, Tim Dunn teaches us that maintaining proper perspective is not only fulfilling, but also provides the strength and wisdom we need to navigate the valleys and mountaintops of our journey here on Earth. Much more than that, however, he reminds us that the way in which we live now will have impact for all of eternity. It is a must read for anyone wanting to make sense out of what appears to be senseless."

Dave Anderson, PhD
President of Grace School of Theology

"*Those who have made an enormous positive impact on the world like Wilberforce, Bonhoeffer, and Luther viewed life with a perspective shaped by God's word and leading. In this short book, Dunn demonstrates how any believer can make the same choice and argues persuasively that God's promise for each of us is that any life lived from a true, God-shaped perspective is heroic from God's perspective.*"

Greg Thornbury
Chancellor, The King's College

"*Choosing a true perspective is one of the most important things an individual can do in their life. It sounds easy, but in the most difficult times, it is anything but easy. Through a very personal story, Tim Dunn teaches the reader how to choose a true perspective and how to trust God, even when it might feel like you can't. I was privileged to be with Tim and his family during this very difficult time, so I have a more intimate perspective on this book than most. I can assure any reader that this is the real deal. What I witnessed as this family dealt with the most terrible tragedy imaginable was the choice of a true perspective and a trust in God like nothing I have ever personally witnessed. Being a witness, and now reading this book, have both strengthened my faith in God and my personal commitment to choosing a true perspective.*"

Mark Meckler
President, Citizens for Self-Governance, and the
Convention of States Project

"In Yellow Balloons, *Tim Dunn reminds us it is not what we know about God that matters. What matters is that we know God personally* by faith, *and that we let Him love us through all our trials and suffering. Through his own Job-like experience, Tim shares his journey into a place where we can see God and know him in a much deeper way than ever before. It is a journey you can take with him by reading* Yellow Balloons. *I promise it will not disappoint."*

Jim DeMint
Former U.S. Senator and Senior Advisor to Convention of States

"Ok, so this is my dad's book, and I just might be a bit biased. But our relationship doesn't change the loss we experienced as a family. Yellow Balloons *tells that story. It will challenge you. It will instruct you. It will inspire you. It will give you the hope and the humility to handle whatever comes your way."*

David Dunn
BEC recording artist of the *Yellow Balloons* album and hit songs "Wanna Go Back" and "Today Is Beautiful"

"For the past thirty years, I have worked as a management consultant, advising senior executives on how to best achieve their desired results. I've learned through the years that successful executives have a true perspective and a vivid and detailed understanding of where they want to take their organization, as well as the actions required to get there. In Yellow Balloons, *Tim Dunn offers a compelling and practical guide to achieving the right outlook in life and successfully navigating the ups and downs that are sure to come—an excellent resource for getting where you need to go."*

Thomas Elsenbrook
Managing Director, Alvarez & Marsal's Corporate Performance Improvement

"How can I be a Christian in this rough world we live in? Grace, courage, and forgiveness aren't relevant unless they suffuse our lives outside of church. Yellow Balloons *offers a profound answer to what that means and how to do it."*

Leslie Graves
President of Ballotpedia.org

"This book is a complete game-changer. It is one thing to know the Scriptures, which Tim does better than most pastors I know, but it is another thing to apply God's Word to the rugged realities of everyday living. And it is yet another thing to have your heart shredded by the inconsolable grief of losing your beloved granddaughter at such an early age—and then to be able to put one faltering foot in front of the next and continue walking God's appointed path. Many believers, even strong ones, never manage to do that. Tim shows us in no uncertain terms what it truly means to live life under the sway and spell of an eternal perspective. Thank you, Tim, for letting us in on the raw, unedited, authentic details of your journey, and then pointing us to the Scriptures and the One lurking behind those Scriptures. I have no doubt that anyone reading this book will find themselves drawn to Jesus, very possibly as never before."

Dwight Edwards
Best-selling author and founder of *Revolution Within* ministries

DEDICATION

On September 18, 2015, my twenty-two-month-old granddaughter Moriah Constance Wimberly was called into the arms of Jesus while she slept. Her favorite color was yellow, so my wife (her "Mimi") wore a yellow dress to the memorial service, where we ate lemon cake and drank lemonade. After the service, we released yellow balloons into the sky. Because they were beautiful, yet out of sight in just a few moments, they were a fitting tribute to Moriah's short life.

We didn't get to say a proper goodbye, so I hope this book creates a lasting memory of her, while demonstrating how to make some sense of events we really can't explain.

This book is dedicated as a memorial to Moriah and a testimony to how our lives can be blessed by choosing a true perspective.

FOREWORD

Every now and then you come across a commentary that explains clearly, in a straightforward format, what life is really about. *Yellow Balloons* is such a book.

Yellow Balloons is a wonderful insight into relationship with our Creator, our family, our fellow employees, and also with ourselves and our perspective as outlined by Jesus Himself. In John 17:3 Jesus said "this is eternal life that you would KNOW the one true God and Christ whom he has sent." His kingdom has come. He sent the Holy Spirit to be our Helper.

Tim Dunn becomes transparent and shares his story of personal loss, misplaced priorities, and his personal spiritual path. The "What did I do to deserve this?" "Why me?" and even "What could I have done?" are addressed as he takes us through creating perspectives that are scripturally based and applicable to all of us.

A.W. Tozer taught about thinking rightly about God. Tim Dunn teaches us the "how-to" in that thinking. We are all on a short journey through this life, and the experience and learning shared by Tim will challenge us to truly know the One true God. He shares that perspective, the perspective in relationship to the ONE TRUE GOD, no matter your situation, will give your life meaning regardless of circumstance.

Tim causes us to think in the now with the Holy Spirit as our partner in this journey. He relates to me at age seventy and he relates well how to live that journey, whether on the highest mountaintop, or in the depths of the valley, or on the plains where we most often find ourselves.

This is a book for everyone who would like to lift burdens and have relationship in every aspect of the journey called LIFE. A journey that is relationship with His Helper.

- Former U.S. Senator, Tom Coburn

CONTENTS

1

THAT DAY

My wife and I raised our six children in what has been described as "the capital of the West Texas oil patch," Midland, Texas. Because the economy revolves around petroleum—and not much else—we've lived through boom and bust periods. On a roll, Midland has some of the highest per capita income in the country; people drive around in new cars and build big houses. At the height of a boom cycle, my business partner came in one day and said he had seen a highly tatted rig hand pull in to a convenience store parking lot in a Lamborghini.

High wages draw most available workers into the oil field, and many restaurants have to turn away eager patrons due to a lack of waitstaff. Due to a lack of available housing, "man camps" pop up all over. (A man camp is a dirt parking lot covered by small sheds, RVs, and trailers.) And since the oil field runs 24/7, a lot of roommates practice "hot bedding," where another worker is ready to sleep in your bed as soon as you leave for work.

While many banks across America have electronic signs outside their buildings announcing the temperature or the time, one local bank has a sign that tells passersby the current per-barrel price of oil. OPEC meetings make newspaper headlines in Midland. During the bust periods, however, drilling rigs sit idle, parking lots are filled with unused company vehicles, and laid-off geologists cross-train to become stockbrokers and move to Dallas.

In contrast to the more fertile, eastern areas of the state, West Texas is semi-arid. If you see a grove of trees, it almost always is shading a home because most trees don't grow without irrigation. West Texas has some beautiful areas—Big Bend National Park, for example—but Midland pretty much has all the ugly and none of the beauty; sandstorms but no river. We're surrounded by flatland covered in unattractive mesquite bushes. Even so, I love the town, because it's full of hard-working entrepreneurs who embody the pioneer spirit of those who settled the American West. Life is mainly about the people you interact with rather than the landscape you view, and the Midland community is something I really love.

The one exception to ugly-all-around is the West Texas sky. The low humidity sky is a beautiful, expansive blue. The sunsets can be breathtaking and the stars amazing. The clouds are awe-inspiring, particularly when afternoon thunderstorms gather. Although so much beauty is directly overhead, it's often missed. To appreciate it, you have to look up. Perhaps that's part of what shapes Midland's entrepreneurial culture.

I grew up in Big Spring, Texas, just about forty miles northeast of Midland. I'm thankful that five of my six children have returned to West Texas now that they're grown, married, and have children of their own. (I have fifteen grandchildren and counting.) My wife and I get to have a lot of quality *and* quantity time with them, which we wouldn't have if they were spread out all over the nation.

Our daughter Mary Kathryn and her husband (like me, named Tim) moved to Midland at the height of an oil boom when few houses were available. So in January 2015, they moved in with us. Eventually they found a fixer-upper just a few houses down from our son Wally and his wife, Micah. Mary Kathryn and Tim extended their stay with us while they remodeled their house. It was fun to have their little daughters running around. Wheatly had just turned three and Moriah was only fourteen months. Wheatly was tall; Moriah was a little thing who more than made up for her size with a curious fearlessness. We enjoyed watching her change from a baby into a toddler as she learned to communicate in one-word sentences. Moriah was a compassionate kid, the kind who would cry if she saw someone else get hurt. It was awesome to get to know the details of the grandkids' lives on a day-to-day basis.

Although five of our grown children decided to return to work in the oil business, one took a different path. Our son David graduated from Texas Tech (a hundred miles from Midland) with an engineering degree. He could easily have gone the petroleum route, but what he really loved was playing the acoustic scene in Lubbock. When it was time to take a job, he decided to launch a music career instead of taking a high-paying engineering job; he said he didn't want to look back on his life and wonder if he could have made it. Consistent with his entrepreneurial heritage, he launched a career in music with his guitar and voice as his only assets.

Pretty soon, he appeared on the television show *The Voice*. Though he didn't win, he took off to Nashville to pursue his singing career. Now he's a thousand miles from Midland but never far from our hearts and minds, especially when we hear his songs on the radio. When little Moriah would hear his voice coming through our car radio, she'd squeal, "Days!" (Translation: "Uncle David!"). Then she'd start dancing or clapping along to his music.

In addition to loving to belt out David's songs, Moriah enjoyed eating dessert and going to parties. She loved our frequent family get-togethers, as she'd perfected the skill of "lap surfing": picking out the family members who had the best food on their plates and asking them to share . . . just a bite.

When she knew we were getting together, she'd exclaim, "Cake!" Moriah had a limited vocabulary, but she knew the words that mattered.

Like her Uncle David, Moriah was a daredevil. But her courage was accompanied by clumsiness. Often I would catch little Moriah precariously balanced, with one knee on the couch and one foot on the coffee table. It sometimes resulted in an owie but wouldn't make Moriah more cautious.

In September 2015 when David came to town for the first time in months to play a concert, he and I stopped by to see Moriah. That day she'd gone with her mother to drop off her older sister at school and had heard David's song on the radio on the way home.

"Days!" she exclaimed, happy to hear her uncle's song even though she was running a fever. Her mother smiled at the little voice coming from the back seat. Moriah couldn't say all the words to the song, so she sang the end of each phrase. "Eyes . . . light . . . sky . . ."

"Want to go see Uncle David?" Mary Kathryn asked. But by the time David and I got to see her,

Moriah was in Mary Kathryn's arms feeling poorly and in no mood to play.

"Blanket," she said. "Nap."

"I think she just needs to sleep," Mary Kathryn explained. We said our goodbyes, and David and I climbed into my truck and headed out for a tour of our new office building. We chatted as we drove and barely noticed the ambulance that passed us as we turned on to Big Spring Street.

My phone rang. Not much time had passed since we left the house, so I wasn't expecting the tone of Terri's voice. We'd been married thirty-eight years at the time, so as soon as I heard her I knew something was very wrong.

"Come home now. Moriah is unresponsive." she said.

David remembers what happened next a little differently than I do. The way he tells it, we walked into our house and saw Terri with blood all over the front of her shirt. I don't remember that detail. I knew Moriah was prone to fever-induced seizures, but the condition wasn't supposed to be life-threatening. Mary Kathryn just kept a close eye on her, which is exactly what she was doing when she noticed something wrong during her daughter's nap.

Mary Kathryn had put Moriah down for a nap in a room next to her bathroom, so she could check on her often. One time when she went in to check on her, she noticed that Moriah was blue. Terri had gone for a walk and had just returned to the house when she heard Mary Kathryn yelling for her. Terri ran in and immediately administered CPR. Moriah had spit up blood; her heart had stopped.

The paramedics, who arrived in minutes, whisked her away to the hospital. Terri already had gotten Moriah to regain her normal color, so she was hopeful they could start her heart again. But later we learned that young children almost never respond to a heart restart; it only works about ten percent of the time.

When David and I got to the house we learned that the ambulance that had passed us, sirens blazing, contained my daughter Mary Kathryn and little Moriah. When the police showed up at the house, Terri and I stayed to answer their questions. Before we were done, one of the officers said, "We're sorry to tell you that your granddaughter did not make it." By the time we got to the hospital to be with Mary Kathryn, the private room the hospital had provided was packed full of friends and family, all crying. Mary Kathryn looked up at us and said, through her tears, "Her heart just wouldn't start again."

Moriah's pediatrician assured her parents there was nothing they could've done differently to save her life. But as we stood there crying, our close-knit family was faced with a choice.

What perspective would we choose to have about this sudden tragedy?

2

THE ANGELS ARE WATCHING

How do you describe grief? It's like describing pain. In spite of all our modern technology, hospitals still use degrees of sad faces for us to describe how much pain we have. When Moriah died, I felt like my soul had been knocked out in a boxing match and I was having trouble coming to. I could recognize the fog of grief; after sixty years of living, I had known it before. But this was a harder gut punch than most. I knew I needed help getting up off the mat; the entire family would need help. If we didn't choose the right perspective, this unavoidable disaster would become the first of many avoidable ones.

God sent help immediately when our pastor stopped by the house after we got home from the hospital. As we sat in the living room, I asked him, "How can we avoid becoming part of the high percentage of people whose relationships fall apart after a tragedy?"

He talked to us about healthy ways to grieve and warned that Moriah's death could separate us if we didn't learn to grieve well. Instead of trying to avoid the pain of grief, he encouraged us to embrace grief. Yes, he said *embrace,* but added that grief is something that needs to be shared. If you think about it, it makes sense that grieving together brings togetherness and avoiding one another to avoid the pain of grief pulls us apart.

He gave us advice on how to handle it if one of us was having a good day while another family member wasn't. "Step into their grief and grieve with them the way they prefer to grieve," our pastor told us. "It'll ruin your day but cement your relationship." He pointed out that couples who lose a child often get divorced. To avoid being separated by grief, resist the urge to "get over" the tragedy or to simply look on the bright side. Rather, realize the importance of grief.

Jesus grieved, after all. I still grieve over Moriah's death. But our pastor's words helped me develop the perspective that grieving is an investment in our remaining relationships. And that perspective has grown and evolved to something much more, something much deeper.

When you think about it, there is precious little that we can control. We can't control whether a little girl's heart keeps beating. Our worrying won't affect the future. In David Kuhnert's excellent book *Servant Leadership*, he explains that we can control only three things: whom we trust, what we do, and the perspective we choose in any situation. That last one, our perspective, shapes and molds how we interpret things that happen to and around us. Perspective also influences the decisions we make. Here's the crazy thing: most of us choose a perspective without realizing it. Of roughly eight billion people in the world, we get to decide the perspective and actions of exactly one. That's why each of us should be very intentional about the perspective we choose every moment of every day.

Most of our family participated in a Grief Share class at church. I read the materials, since I learn better that way. Most if not all of us heeded the advice to step into the grief. For me, stepping into grief included a long series of interactions with a large number of friends and acquaintances, including many acquaintances from the oil and gas business. We've been in Midland more than thirty years, so I know a lot of people. When someone approached me, I knew what was coming, I needed to talk about Moriah's death again, and the bandage would be torn off that wound yet again.

Our pastor's advice continually reminded me I had a choice. I could defer pain and push people away, or I could embrace pain and allow others to grieve with me. I could view each opportunity to tear off the Band-Aid as an investment in others and an opportunity to accelerate rather than defer healing. My friends wanted to grieve too. Of course, their grief is much smaller. But although it hurt a lot when I stepped into the grief with them, I tried to consider it a worthwhile investment in those excellent friendships. It is a tough choice to make; there was nothing comfortable or easy about it then, and it is still difficult. But like any good investment, it pays in time. Gradually the intense ache of grief was soothed by the love of so many friends.

Most of us don't deliberately look at a range of perspectives and then, after careful consideration, adopt one. For most of my life I didn't act in this intentional way, and my life suffered for it. My relationship with Terri is deeper now because of Moriah. But who knows what might have transpired had a tragedy such as this occurred years ago, or if we hadn't listened to such wise guidance?

Rather than living *above* our circumstances by choosing a true perspective up front, we tend instead to live *under* the circumstances. That leads us to be victims of our circumstances. A victim is someone without a choice. When we merely react, we allow circumstances to control us. There is a better way. We can make choices based on our core values and our life objectives. By deliberately choosing a true perspective, we can make choices *in spite* of circumstances. And when we learn this skill, we can begin to see that circumstances are, in fact, simply the environment in which we operate. We become like surfers, and circumstances are the waves upon which we surf.

Choosing a true perspective does not eliminate pain. In fact, as with stepping into grief, it might even accelerate pain and worsen it for a time. But it is an important step in grappling with the questions that attend the intense pain brought by suffering. If we don't get satisfactory answers to questions such as "Why me?" and "Why would a loving God allow this?" the pain can spiral into debilitation and dysfunction. (I had a brush with such a circumstance twenty years earlier. More on that soon.)

Choosing a true perspective was the key for Dorothy in *The Wizard of Oz*. Dorothy didn't realize she already possessed the ability to escape her victimhood until the Good Witch of the North taught her how to close her eyes, click her heels, and think, *There's no place like home.* When we learn to deliberately choose a true perspective, it's like Dorothy learning to click her heels. It's transformative, liberating, and empowering. It frees us. But Dorothy wasn't ready to hear that message until she had first endured numerous trials. Likewise, as we learn to "click our heels," we will have to tangle with some very hard truths.

For example, since God is God He could have kept Moriah from dying. You can undoubtedly insert the name of your loved one(s) in that sentence. Or you might ask why God didn't keep someone from getting cancer or from having a professional setback or suffering financial woes. And you'd be right to ask. Struggling through these questions is a necessary first step to developing our true perspective.

We frequently try to get God to alter our circumstances. Some of us even try to "punish" God by deciding to not believe in Him following a tragic event. There's a better way to respond in the face of tragedy, but it requires a pretty radical shift: we can *trust* that God has our best interests at heart. Yes, always. Though "In God We Trust" is engraved on our coins, it's more than just a slogan. It's not easy to trust God, especially during a tragedy. But that is where a true perspective will eventually lead us.

Our first step in grappling with these major perspective-setting questions will be to explore why God left us on this imperfect planet in the first place.

Our Opportunity

Sometimes we think of heaven as a place where everything is possible. But I was astonished when I discovered the biblical teaching that we have an opportunity *on Earth* that we won't have in heaven. What is it that we can do here but won't be able to do there?

The answer lies in two verses of Scripture that explain that angels are watching us, even carefully studying us. Ephesians 3:10 tells us: "[N]ow the manifold wisdom of God might be made known *by the church to the principalities and powers in the heavenly places*." That means the angels are watching us to understand the wisdom of God.

Then in 1 Peter 1:12, we are told, "[T]he gospel [was sent] to you by the Holy Spirit . . . from heaven—things which *angels* desire to look into . . ." The phrase "look into" conveys the notion of an archeologist studying an artifact with intense curiosity. The angels are fascinated by looking into our lives and seeing human history play out. They're watching us with the intensity of a movie-goer immersed in a particularly riveting movie.

But what's so special about our lives that these mighty beings would venture from heaven to carefully investigate and learn from us? What's going on down here that's decidedly not going on up there?

Faith. Faith in God is something angels don't have. In fact, angels *can't* walk by faith. Faith is believing something we can't see or otherwise verify with our physical senses. Once we get to heaven, we will share this condition with the angels, we will no longer be able to have faith in God. Like the angels, we'll know God firsthand. Since living by faith is not something angels can experience, they're longing to see it in action on Earth. That's why they are intensely studying us, and in doing so learning about the wisdom of God.

Your life and mine are grand dramas. Our lives—and any person's life on Earth—tell a story that supersedes *Spider-Man, Cinderella, Lord of the Rings,* or whatever epic tale has captured your imagination. Every one of us is intended to play a leading role, but we get to choose whether to take the part. (More on this in Chapter 7.) If we don't choose the right perspective, we may miss our chance. Our lives on Earth are a very short, spectacularly amazing, once-in-an-existence opportunity. The angels are watching, studying us, because it is an opportunity they'll never experience firsthand.

At least part of the reason God leaves us here in flawed bodies on this flawed earth, a place filled with death and misery, is because of an amazing benefit that we can gain *only here*, in this life. Our capacity to enjoy this world as well as the world to come will be immensely expanded or diminished by the choices we make during our lives on Earth. Without a true perspective we can lose out on the phenomenal opportunity our lives afford us. When we embrace the amazing, one-time opportunity this life offers, we will also come to realize that the choices we make will dent eternity.

Here's an earthly example how a true perspective can lead to happiness in this life. My wife and I took our kids and grandkids to Disneyland, often described as "the happiest place on Earth." As we chatted with one of the workers at the Snow White's Scary Adventures ride, we discovered things there aren't always as happy as the glossy advertisements portray.

"I'd say at least half the young kids emerge from this ride in tears," we were told by the Disneyland attendant at the Snow White ride who responded to our question. It turns out our grandkids are pretty typical.

In other words, this two-minute, theme-park ride only brings joy to the kids who have a more mature perspective. They realize the scary witch character isn't part of the real world. They can enjoy the epic adventure without worrying that Snow White is a real princess in danger of perishing. They know their own fate isn't controlled by dark forces. They aren't victims. They know they'll quickly be back outside in the sunshine, eating funnel cakes and cotton candy and having a great time.

They have a perspective that is rooted in reality. The younger children don't. They can't get above what appears to be frightening circumstances on the ride.

We have the opportunity to believe what the Bible tells us about life being like a two-minute ride. Our lives on Earth are a brief sojourn prior to arriving at our eternal home when our scary adventure will be over. As the book of James puts it, ". . . For what is your life? It is even a vapor that appears for a little time and then vanishes away" (James 4:14). Our days on Earth are but a wisp of smoke against the skyline of eternity. As American abolitionist John Brown said, "There is an eternity behind and an eternity before, and the little speck in the centre, however long, is but comparatively a minute."[1] Also, like a theme-park ride, everyone's earthly life takes twists and turns, ups and downs, before our sojourn here ends. This is the common lot of all humanity. Life is, in fact, a great adventure.

Yes, our lives are a grand drama, an epic saga. Unlike the brief, make-believe world of Snow White's Scary Adventures, the ride of life is real, and it has astronomically high stakes. It is a quest. Although God has provided a certain "happily ever after" ending for us to embrace, and happiness and heroic adventure are proper companions, without the proper perspective we can miss the happiness and cry all through the ride.

Life on Earth is brief in contrast to eternity, but it's an epic tale with cosmic consequences. Still, it's easy for us to misunderstand the stakes. Our earthly sojourn will take us through a wide assortment of experiences, challenges, and opportunities, all skillfully designed by our loving Father to help us become the men and women He created us to be. If we learn to see these experiences for what they really are—in other words, if we adopt a perspective that is real and true—then life will begin to make sense no matter the circumstances.

When we say, "Well, we just need to trust God," we often mean "I'll trust God to bail me out when I really need help." That's not what the Bible talks about. Our great opportunity is to trust God when things *don't* make sense, when life grinds to a halt in a desperate place. Like trusting a fellow soldier in a foxhole, this creates a bond that cannot be recreated elsewhere. One of the greatest rewards for people who trust God in life's foxholes will be that they know God in a way others don't and never will. Those who "overcome" in this way are like veterans who fought in a war together and meet years later at a reunion. Visitors can listen to the soldiers reminisce, but they never can be a part of that exclusive club.

Thankfully, the severe circumstances of loss and suffering are only one part of the terrain of our journey. The terrain of life varies dramatically in scope and nature. It basically falls into three categories: the valleys, the plains, and the mountaintops.

First, we will explore the valleys.

3

PERSPECTIVE IN THE VALLEY

Most of us want to avoid the valley. It's a place of shadows, a place where less of the sky is visible. But there is perspective to be gained in the valley that can't be gained elsewhere.

More than twenty years ago, I had a business disagreement with someone who was, and still is, a friend. I'd been really successful in the oil and gas industry—becoming an executive when I was twenty-seven years old. I'd already lost my bulletproof vest when I survived a severe depression in oil prices; I'd learned industry swings hurt everyone alike. Still, when I looked around, almost everyone at my level was much older. I was flying pretty high. I enjoyed a nice income and had some excellent investments and a lot of prestige. From my perspective, things were going great.

Then, my lofty view of myself was destroyed when this business disagreement ended up causing my friend and me to part ways, and with it an end to the security of regular employment. During that same season, I lost my dad to cancer. On top of all that, in the midst of the business disagreement, my friend told me, "You are generally viewed as arrogant. You don't acknowledge people, and you use intimidation to get your way."

He didn't exactly follow the biblical admonition to correct a brother gently, but the accusation still hit home. I realized that I would stomp on people without even noticing or caring in order to get things done. I wanted accomplishment more than I wanted to properly regard people's feelings and perspectives. I was a self-a-holic.

I also realized I wanted to be in control, but without taking responsibility. Consequently, I wasn't really the kind of leader or person I aspired to be, or the kind God called me to be. Suddenly, it was as if all the rejection I'd caused others to feel over time was gathered together and then delivered to me all at once. I felt cut to the core.

I realized that I am, in fact, an arrogant jerk. Although this admission occurred now over twenty years ago, I say "am" arrogant because my base nature, what the Bible calls my "flesh" hasn't really changed; my instincts are still selfish. When I make this admission to others they sometimes reply that they haven't seen that in me, which just means that the times they have been around me I have successfully walked apart from or masked that base nature. This is an important part of my current reality, a true perspective about myself. I sometimes say my personality profile is that I am a J-E-R-K.

Some companies actually seek out arrogant people when looking for prospective CEOs, possibly because arrogant leaders are good at getting things done. That sort of "leadership" ultimately serves self, however, not the mission of the company or organization. (To see the dysfunction this causes, look no further than a television comedy such as *The Office*.)

As I realized and admitted my failure, God demolished me. Then He brought people into my life to show me how to be the person I really wanted to be. At first, though, I just knew the intense emotion of profound failure. I slipped into depression as I searched for answers. Though my life on the outside retained all the appearances of success, inwardly it was an emotional hurricane. *Why me? What is life about? Why all this pain? Why can't I just live a comfortable life and then go to heaven?*

Why does failure or rejection hurt so much? During a recent TED Talk, Guy Winch explained that our brains register pain in response to rejection. "When scientists placed people in functional MRI machines and asked them to recall a recent rejection, they discovered something amazing. The same areas of our brain become activated when we experience rejection as when we experience physical pain. That's why even small rejections hurt more than we think they should, because they elicit literal (albeit, emotional) pain."[2]

I can certainly testify to his findings. All these years later, I still remember how much this experience hurt. It was an experience I would never request. Still, I'm grateful for what it taught me. The pain I felt during that period really was a sort of death—the death of my lofty self-image.

I searched for answers in a lot of places but ended up finding them in the biblical book of Job. I now feel like Job is one of my best friends. It's like he reached down and lifted me out of the pit. Job's story has since had a special significance for me. Through Job, I began to see myself in an honest and true way. Sounds good, right? Well, it is, but not in a way that made the pain stop immediately. During the first stage of this process, my self-rationalizations were shattered, along with my false self-image. It hurt like crazy.

Job's experiences taught me how to be happy in spite of great pain. (Even when, as in the case of my arrogance, it was self-inflicted.) When Moriah died years later, it was a different kind of grief since I hadn't caused the problem. However, the lessons I had learned while reading the book of Job during my existential crisis helped prepare me to deal with her death. Job gave me a peace that borrows its happiness from another day and another time, which is a perspective born not of this world. It's a peace that comes from knowing this: God is good even when circumstances aren't, and God left us here on this painful earth for a deeply profound and beneficial reason.

Though the book of Job was, at first, jolting, I now find it to be a comforting explanation for what's really going on when we suffer. Pour some coffee and let its richness wash over you, while I tell you how Job changed my life.

A Conversation

The book of Job opens with an unusual scene—a conversation between God and Satan in heaven. This is not a heaven with puffy clouds, harps, and cherubs; it's more like a reception room, maybe like the Oval Office. The sons of God— that is, the angels—come to give an account of themselves. Satan is a fallen angel and, consistent with what we have already learned about angels, the topic of conversation is a human they have been watching.

"From where do you come?" God asks Satan.

"From going to and fro on the earth," he

replies, "and from walking back and forth on it."

"Have you considered my servant Job," God asks, "that there is none like him on the earth, a blameless and upright man, one who fears God and shuns evil?"

God most assuredly isn't trying to get information. He's omniscient, after all. Instead, He's mocking the evil one. It's as if God is taunting Satan. "Have you looked closely at this human being who, of his own free will, does what you were supposed to do?" It's divine trash talk. "Job's my main man; he's the best and puts you to shame. Will you admit it?"

Satan does some trash talking of his own. "Does Job fear God for nothing?" he taunts. "Have You not made a hedge around him, around his household, and around all that he has on every side?" Satan's basic charge is that Job is just a shrewd trader. Job isn't all that righteous; Job just understands a good bargain. Give God what He wants, you get what you want in return.

"You've given him everything," Satan is saying. Just look at Job's big family and his security and wealth. Job, basically an ancient billionaire, was the richest man alive at that time. Beyond his riches, he'd been given ten children, a monumental blessing in that age and culture. Job had more possessions than he could ever need. He owned sheep (ranching), camels (trade), and productive land for farming. In our economy this would be like owning an agribusiness conglomerate, plus trucking and railroad interests, and a banking and trading operation. What more could Job want?

"Of course he's playing ball," Satan taunts God. "You met all his salary demands. Given what You pay, he'd be a fool not to do what You ask."

So what does God do? He tells Satan to go ahead and have his way with Job, only not to lay a hand on his body. In doing this, *God removed the hedge of protection.* Satan wreaks havoc on Job's possessions and his family. In one day, all of Job's possessions are plundered, his servants are murdered, and all of his sons and daughters are killed. The way Satan arranged it, there could be no doubt it was supernatural. Satan did everything he could to let Job know, "No more goodies, your deal is over. God won't give you what you want any more."

What does Job do? He strips himself naked, shaves his head, and falls to the ground. He puts dust on his head, an ancient way of mourning. Then, Job . . . "worshipped. And he said: 'Naked I came from my mother's womb, and naked shall I return there. The lord gave, and the lord has taken away; blessed be the name of the lord.'" Nothing could have been a greater repudiation of Satan's accusation against Job.

Here is perspective we need to gain from the valley. Job captured it well. "I will gratefully accept whatever God brings me; it is His prerogative. He gave me life in the first place, and all I have came from Him. If He wants it back, it is His to take." This was not at all what Satan had predicted. And to make things worse for Satan, Job even *worshipped.*

Worship in the Bible includes simply saying something that is true about God. Job isn't pretending to be happy, he's just saying he gratefully accepts what God is doing. In this respect Job trusts God and already has the correct perspective. But there's much more to learn.

The final verse of Job chapter 1 says: "In all this Job did not sin nor charge God with wrong." Imagine the angels' surprise and delight watching this battle play out in front of them. Not only did Job not curse God to His face, as Satan predicted, but Job worshipped God. Score: God 1, Satan 0.

Satan Returns

If Satan is anything, he's relentless. Scene two in heaven is almost an exact rerun of scene one, but with two notable exceptions. First, God now has more material with which to mock Satan. "Then the Lord said to Satan, 'Have you considered My servant Job, that there is none like him on the earth, a blameless and upright man, one who fears God and shuns evil?'" Then God adds: "And still he holds fast to his integrity, although you incited Me against him, to destroy him without cause."

Note that God takes responsibility here for Job's ruin. While Satan actually did it, God authorized it. In both the books of Job and Revelation, God authorizes every terrible episode, many of which involve Satan's wreaking havoc on Earth. But Satan is always subservient to God's sovereign purposes, even if Satan mistakenly believes he's winning.

God again permits Satan to test whether Job's obedience is simply a way for Job to get what he wants from God. And this time, the test targets Job's health. "So Satan answered the Lord and said, 'Skin for skin! Yes, all that a man has he will give for his life. But stretch out Your hand now, and touch his bone and his flesh, and he will surely curse You to Your face!' And the Lord said to Satan, 'Behold, he is in your hand, but spare his life'" (Job 2:4–6).

Satan leaves. (You can almost hear him chuckling.) Then Satan strikes Job with boils—painful, oozing, feverish open wounds—from the soles of his feet to the crown of his head. Job takes a piece of broken pottery and sits in a heap of ashes to scrape his boils. Even Job's wife comes to test him. "Do you still hold fast to your integrity?" she asks him in bitterness. "Curse God and die!" I guess now we know one reason Satan spared Job's wife: so she could add insult to injury. Job's wife became yet another instrument that Satan used to tempt Job.

Through it all, Job shows incredible grace. "You speak as one of the foolish women speaks. Shall we indeed accept good from God, and shall we not accept adversity?" He doesn't say, "You're a fool!" Instead he tells her, "When you talk like that and ask me to curse God, you *sound* foolish." Even through all his adversity, Job remains gracious in the face of his wife's scathing rebuke. God speaks highly of Job for good reason. Perhaps the good angels watching the drama unfold all stood and applauded as the new score was posted: God, 2. Satan, 0.

But an interesting sentence closes this episode. "In all this Job did not sin with his lips." This becomes important as we consider the unhelpful advice Job is about to hear from his friends.

With Friends Like These . . .

As the story of Job continues to unfold, Job's three friends come to comfort him. These guys are truly friends. They sit with Job in mourning for seven solid days before they say anything. (It was ancient custom to let the aggrieved speak first.) *Seven days.* Would you do that? Not me.

But once Job starts speaking, an extensive dialogue ensues. Through the rest of the book of Job their counsel essentially comes down to this: Job, these bad things came upon you because you have sinned. Confess and repent, and God will restore your losses. "If you would earnestly seek God and make your supplication to the Almighty, if you were pure and upright, surely now He would awake for you, and prosper your rightful dwelling place. Though your beginning was small, yet your latter end would increase abundantly."

You'd think Job would embrace this simple formula. "Confess, and it will go away" sounds awesome. But there's one problem, as we learned already from God. Job is a man of the utmost integrity. He knows of no sins, or certainly he would've already repented. His friends insist that Job should just give God what He wants so Job could be restored and get what he wants.

Job refuses.

Then God slams the friends' advice. Speaking to the first friend, Eliphaz, God declares, "My wrath is aroused against you and your two friends, for you have not spoken of Me what is right, as My servant Job has." In other words, God doesn't seem concerned about the friends' unfair criticism of Job, but He blasts them for what they said about *Him*.

Why is God so irritated? Most of what they said about God would pass muster in any church, but it angered God when they basically told Job, "Repent and God will give you the goodies again." Sound familiar? Eliphaz and his two friends are accusing God of being transactional, just like Satan had. Eliphaz, his two friends, Job's wife, and Satan all view God like an idol or a cosmic vending machine. Idolatry always boils down to this: "What price do I have to pay to the 'power' in order to get what I want?" The essence of idolatry is an untrue belief that we actually control our circumstances.

No wonder God is so ticked off. God rebukes them before He really rubs it in. According to their view of God, they should have gotten smacked down like Job had. After all, they had done something hideously wrong and would therefore deserve wrath. But God is not a pay-to-play cosmic mobster. God is God, a God who transcends mere transaction. He's also our very relational and caring Father. Interestingly, God deals pointedly with the friends—by forgiving them—and then lets them off the hook completely. He tells them to ask Job to intercede for them and then simply lets them go. This is exactly the opposite of how they had claimed God operates.

At this point you might think God would give Job a hug and tell him He appreciates his long-suffering. Nope, not yet.

Job's Day in Court

Job perseveres through his trials, steadfastly maintaining his integrity by refusing to treat God as a pay-to-play idol and by refusing to confess sins he knows he didn't commit. But Job does something else. He requests an audience with God. If he could just talk with God, Job reasons, it would give him the opportunity to explain to God how He is misled in this situation. Job seems to think that once God is properly informed, He'll restore Job to better circumstances. Can you identify? I can. This is my natural reflex when things don't go as I wanted. "God, what are you doing? You need to listen to me better." But Job's perspective is about to get an overhaul.

God first made Job the richest man in the world. Now, God is preparing to make Job the richest man in the *universe*. Infinite riches come from listening to God, and Job is about to have the opportunity to listen to God in a manner that is cosmically astonishing. And this perspective-overhaul and infinite wisdom are recorded for us to benefit from as well.

> "Oh, that I might have my request, that God would grant me the thing that I long for!" (Job 6:8).

> "Teach me, and I will hold my tongue; cause me to understand wherein I have erred" (Job 6:24).

Job, though hurting and miserable, is still righteous. He recognizes that he cannot require answers from the Almighty:

"Truly I know it is so, but how can a man be righteous before God? If one wished to contend with Him, He could not answer Him one time out of a thousand" (Job 9:2–3).

And this:

"If He takes away, who can hinder Him? Who can say to Him, 'What are You doing?'" (Job 9:32).

Although Job fully recognizes God can do as He pleases, he still believes God is mishandling his case:

"See now, I have prepared my case, I know that I shall be vindicated" (Job 13:18).

"Know then that God has wronged me, and has surrounded me with His net" (Job 19:6).

In our age, we might hear a more succinct version of Job's complaint: "How could you let this happen?"

> "Even today my complaint is bitter; my hand is listless because of my groaning. Oh, that I knew where I might find Him, that I might come to His seat! I would present my case before Him, and fill my mouth with arguments. I would know the words which He would answer me and understand what He would say to me. Would He contend with me in His great power? No! But He would take note of me. There the upright could reason with Him, and I would be delivered forever from my Judge" (Job 23:2–7).

In fact, Job does get his day in court. Boy, does he ever. If Satan is relentless, God infinitely more so—but in a wonderful way. God always has our best interest at heart. He wants good for us that infinitely exceeds what a transaction with a manipulatable god could ever provide.

We can rest in this, but only if we adopt the perspective God provides Job, a perspective that allows us to see *above* the circumstances of life.

Not an Explanation, an Explosion

It all begins in Job chapter 38. "Then the Lord answered Job out of the whirlwind, and said: 'Who is this who darkens counsel by words without knowledge? Now prepare yourself like a man; I will question you, and you shall answer Me'" In other words, "Job, I'll be glad to sit before your board of inquiry and answer your demands for satisfactory reasons to explain my actions. But before I answer them, I have just a few pre-trial questions for you."

Question number one: "Where were you when I laid the foundations of the earth? Tell Me, if you have understanding. Who determined its measurements? Surely you know!" No answer? Okay, let's move on.

"Have you commanded the morning since your days began, and caused the dawn to know its place . . . ?

"Have you entered the springs of the sea? Or have you walked in search of the depths? Have the gates of death been revealed to you? Have you comprehended the breadth of the earth? Tell Me, if you know all this."

For the next four chapters, God questions Job about various intricacies of the universe. Philip Yancey, in his book *Where Is God When It Hurts?*, wrote, "When God speaks to Job, He doesn't explain, He explodes. He asks Job who he thinks he is anyway. He says that to try to explain the kind of things Job wants explained would be like trying to explain Einstein to a little neck clam . . . God doesn't reveal His grand design . . . He reveals Himself. The message behind the splendor is, 'Until you know a little about running the physical universe, Job, don't tell me how to run the moral universe.'"[3]

But in all this, please remember—Job is a godly man, the godliest man on Earth. Job is the man God brags about before the heavenly hosts. Job is God's favorite. Many commentaries on the book of Job suggest that Job was somehow inadequate. These commentaries may suggest that we should avoid being like Job. But as I studied and identified with Job and his pain, in circumstances much worse than mine, I came to greatly admire him.

He's heroic. Job was far more godly and righteous than I, and he suffered much, much more than I did.

His life example still provides a life-changing lesson for me. Why would a loving God allow such horrific things to occur to His favorite guy? Because God saw an enormous, untapped opportunity for Job. God doesn't want His favorite guy to miss out on any enduring benefits he could gain from his brief sojourn on Earth.

> "Then Job answered the Lord and said: 'I know that You can do everything, and that no purpose of Yours can be withheld from You. You asked, "Who is this who hides counsel without knowledge?" Therefore I have uttered what I did not understand, things too wonderful for me, which I did not know. Listen, please, and let me speak; You said, "I will question you, and you shall answer Me." I have heard of You by the hearing of the ear, but now my eye sees You. Therefore I abhor myself, and repent in dust and ashes'"

(Job 42:1–6). And as Job had previously concluded, "I am vile" (Job 40:4).

Job already had the best and truest perspective of any human in the story. But God overhauled and expanded Job's perspective in a dramatic way. As a result, Job came to know God and could trust God as never before. Job came to know God by faith as never before. And knowing God by faith is something we can gain only in this life. This same benefit will not be available to us beyond our earthly life's two-minute adventure ride.

Job humbled himself before God as never before, because real humility is simply seeing things truly. Job initially thought God was missing perspective. It turns out Job was the one who was missing perspective. It was a long and bloody road, but God truly brought His choice servant into a far wealthier place.

Infinite riches come from "buying gold" from God as we listen to Him and understand Him (as we can see from Revelation 3:18–20). Job now, by faith, ascends to a whole new level of understanding in this life and of eternal riches in the next life.

Job now sees God not just as a power who can do as He pleases, but as the One who sees all things truly. Job now knows God's perspective is unlimited and true, and Job's relationship to God now seems intimate. Job now understands that his perspective is limited and wanting. God has taken His favorite servant to a place where Job can know God *by faith*. Job has gained a treasure the spectating angels cannot experience firsthand.

Though I couldn't fully identify with Job's horrific circumstances, I could completely identify with Job's pain. Also, I identified with what Job said after his encounter with God. "I am vile" (Job 40:4). I don't know if Job concluded he was an arrogant jerk, but he definitely altered his self-image. The ultra-successful Job now saw himself as very small.

When I thought about how I sought control and stepped on people while accomplishing business goals, God said to me, "Here, I'll let you see yourself for who you really are and see me for who I really am." It was then I reached the same conclusion about myself: "I am vile." This was a far different perspective of myself than I had ever had before. There's a world of difference between saying, "I don't have it all together" and recognizing inescapably, "I am vile." Based on my study of the Hebrew word translated "vile," I think another valid translation is "small." Job received the great gift of seeing himself truly, as God sees him. "I am not such a hotshot after all." I received a similar gift, and it was one of the more painful, and beneficial, experiences I've ever had.

This experience of reshaping my self-image reminds me of a scene from C. S. Lewis's novel *The Voyage of the Dawn Treader* when the rotten boy named Eustace fell asleep dreaming of riches. When he woke up, he realized he'd turned into a dragon. He felt a pain in his leg because the gold bracelet he'd been wearing as a boy suddenly was too small and constricting on a dragon's leg. His leg hurt, but not as much as the pain of being absolutely alone. He began to cry. Then he remembered dragon skin can be shed like snake skin. He began to claw away his skin only to reveal another deeper layer, and another. Eventually, he tired of the effort. Then Aslan the lion (the Christ figure) makes an offer, "You will have to let me undress you."

Eustace lay on the ground, and here's what happened.

The very first tear he made was so deep that I thought it had gone right into my heart. And when he began pulling the skin off, it hurt worse than anything I've ever felt. The only thing that made me able to bear it was just the pleasure of feeling the stuff peel off . . .

Well, he peeled the beastly stuff right off—just as I thought I'd done it myself the other three times, only they hadn't hurt—and there it was lying on the grass: only ever so much thicker, and darker, and more knobbly-looking than the others had been. And there was I as smooth and soft as a peeled switch and smaller than I had been. Then he caught hold of me—I didn't like that much for I was very tender underneath now that I'd no skin on—and threw me into the water. It smarted like anything but only for a moment. After that it became perfectly delicious and as soon as I started swimming and splashing I found that all the pain had gone from my arm. And then I saw why. I'd turned into a boy again . . .

After a bit the lion took me out and dressed me . . . in new clothes.[4]

When Jesus says to "put sin to death," he means it. I'd read in Romans 7 before, where Paul explains that "no good thing" dwells in our flesh. But now that became a personal reality. I had to turn to God, so He could begin to work on me and to crucify daily the "vile" aspect of my nature. Just as Eustace experienced the dragon skin being torn away, my arrogance and vileness being crucified was excruciatingly painful and liberating at the same time.

It took most of two years for me to recover emotionally, but I was liberated. I no longer had to put on a front. I didn't have to defend my dragon behavior. I didn't have to rationalize any of my words, attitudes, or actions. And I was freed from trying to control the world around me.

Yellow Balloons has its roots in the lessons I learned in my Job-like season. A great burden was lifted. The truth hurt, but it set me free.

God did restore and double the earthly possessions Job lost, but that familial and material wealth paled in comparison to the far greater wealth of deepened intimacy and knowledge, *by faith*, of the unrivaled King of the universe and lover of Job's soul.

God's Best

Shortly after Moriah's death we learned that our daughter Mary Kathryn was pregnant again. We also learned that our daughter-in-law, who had endured eight years of infertility, was to have her long-awaited second child. With these announcements, we cried tears of joy as well as tears of renewed sorrow from missing Moriah. Undoubtedly Job appreciated his improved circumstances, but it takes a true perspective to really become whole on the other side of the valley. Without one, we can't recover sufficiently to enjoy anything on the other side.

As much as we want to think we know best—and that God should be listening more carefully to us—it's just not true. God knows all, so He knows best. God doesn't need more of my perspective; I need more of His. And if God brings us into a difficult circumstance it's for our own good. Only when I began to embrace the pain I experience in life did I start to see and to know what's true, and the freedom it brings. I learned I can look at circumstances as opportunities rather than sources of agitation, which brings a lot of peace.

But still, some really tough questions nagged at me. *Why does it have to be done this way? Why do I need to know God through all this pain? Why not just wait until I get to heaven, then go through 'Knowing God 101'?*

Then God showed me the really big "aha moment." The angels are watching *me* to understand *Him.* That revolutionized my perspective on life, on myself, on what life means. Job was God's favorite guy. Remember, it was *God* who brought up Job in the smack talk with Satan. "See anyone like him?" So if God's favorite guy got this treatment, it must mean that this was the very best thing that could have happened for Job.

God did not want Job to miss one speck of opportunity to know Him by faith. Remember, faith is the one thing we can't do in heaven. God led Job through all the trials, severe as they were, so that His prized servant would not miss out on any blessing knowing Him by faith.

Everyone in the story except Job looked at God as a means to an end, a vehicle to "get what I want." But God is a loving Father who wants what is best for all His children. God knows infinitely better than we do what is good for us, including how to fulfill our deepest desires. In the process of coming to deeply know God by faith, Job came to know himself in a way that was real and true. My perspective, and therefore my life, has been transformed by coming to view circumstances as once-in-an-existence opportunities to know God by faith and to see myself truly. It hasn't made life more comfortable, but it has made it more *meaningful.*

Only God is God. Not me. What a concept! Patently obvious, but practically difficult. So it's not surprising that God would choose to make Job His first written communique to humanity. (Scholars believe the book of Job was written prior to Moses' penning the first five biblical books.)

Job reveals that knowing God is the ultimate experience of life, but it's often tricky, even hazardous, business. If we really want to know God, we will serve Him. In doing so we may experience heartaches that we never thought we would endure. We may be betrayed by people we thought were our closest friends. We may experience losses that seem unbearable. As you know, these are the same sorts of things Jesus experienced. But through these trials, we may enter into the wealthier place of seeing and knowing God as never before. The unlimited gold God offers by listening to Him often can be obtained in huge quantities when our journey takes us through the deepest valleys.

Peace, Even Joy, in a Job-Like Experience
When Moriah died, I lost a business suit.

I have no idea how or where I would've misplaced an entire suit, but grief brings fog. I lived in a daze for some time. Though I had for many years attempted to practice the right perspective, which I learned in Job, I am still a frail human. I was still sad.

I didn't ask God, "Why." But I did still have an unanswered question. Since knowing God by faith is obviously such a huge deal, how will innocent little Moriah gain what she missed because her brief life on Earth was cut short? My answer: I don't know. I know all our lives are short; death is unnatural. A two-year life and an eighty-two-year life both are "wisps of vapor" as God tells us in James 4:14. God leads us to know Him, but unlike what He did with His favorite guy Job, God seldom reveals the intimacies of someone else's story. (The book of Job does not tell us the stories of Job's children, for instance.)

In the days leading up to the time Moriah left us, she took to saying, "Home." Mary Kathryn noticed it and tried to ascertain what she was referring to. Mary Kathryn now thinks God gave Moriah a premonition: she was going home.

Months later, Moriah's dad had a dream that Moriah was playing in heaven with his grandmother who also is there. They were playing with bumblebees, and in heaven bumblebees don't have stingers. I don't know how this is best for Moriah, but I believe it is. Not because of what I know, but because of Whom I know.

I have learned that knowing God by faith is not important only for the next life. It also has a very real and important aspect of *current* happiness. When I understand that what is happening now is shaping me forever, it provides tremendous comfort and even encouragement. The angels are craning their necks to learn about God through our walk of faith. They understand the cosmic importance of our brief sojourn through earthly life. When this life is over, our opportunity to know God by faith will be over forever. At the end of the age when heaven comes down and God dwells personally with us in a New Earth, all tears are wiped away. Maybe many of the tears that will need wiping away will be shed over what we could have gained on Earth had we only walked by faith.

This is our one and only chance to live by faith, so let's grab all the life we can. Thankfully, most of life isn't lived in the depths of despair, it's lived in the normal day-to-day humdrum of existence. However, be warned. This more menial existence, believe it or not, might be even more challenging to live faithfully than the life in the valley.

4

PERSPECTIVE ON THE PLAINS

Much is said about mountaintop experiences, not to mention all the time we spend in the valley. The extremes stand out because they vary from what is typical. So how should we regard all that goes on in between? You and I spend the bulk of our time on "the plains." In the wide-open spaces where we can see from horizon to horizon, the ups and downs appear less significant. And because the plains seem to introduce so few surprises, we tend to consider what happens there to be ordinary. Nothing could be further from the truth.

It was an ordinary Wednesday, but the day was about to become extraordinary.

Moriah, along with her sister and parents, had been living with us for roughly nine months while they shopped for and remodeled their fixer-upper. As a result, Terri and I got to be a big part of Moriah's twenty-two-month life. On this seemingly ordinary Wednesday, Moriah pointed at the back door. With her infectious smile and bright, inquiring eyes shining, she said, "Trampene, trampene." It took me just a second to realize what she was saying.

"Do you want me to take you outside to the trampoline?"

She started to emphatically nod. "Yeah!"

Out to the backyard we went, where I bounced her for a bit. Our trampoline is at ground level, stretched over a hole in the ground to make it kid-friendly. Moriah took advantage of the setup. She went underneath the tarp to play peek-a-boo with me, belly-laughing every time she popped up. We might have been out there twenty minutes.

I could've easily declined the invitation, but I try to say yes when kids ask to play or to have a book read to them, whether I feel like it or not. Why? I've chosen a perspective that reminds me that little things are actually big things. In this instance that brief, special time between Moriah and her Pop Pops was to be my last enduring memory of her. She died two days later.

The moment seemed ordinary at the time because it was, at least in the way we usually think of ordinary. But because Moriah died shortly thereafter, the moment by the trampoline is anything but ordinary to me. Small things are actually big things. This is true even when I have a hard time choosing to embrace that perspective for other events I deem "ordinary." For example, when my four-year-old granddaughter recently asked me to play "Hungry Hungry Hippo," I didn't feel like saying yes. However, I chose to embrace a true perspective that caused me to set up the board and try to get my hippo to gobble up more marbles than hers.

Our heavenly Father considers all His ordinary moments with us children like special times on the "trampene." These are enduring moments that He cherishes and remembers when we think to ask to do life with Him. I sometimes decline children's invitations. I have all sorts of limitations. But God has no limitations, and always He says yes when we ask Him to be with us.

Most of life is not lived in the valley nor on the mountaintop. Most of our existence is not a low or high, an up or a down. Most of our time on Earth is lived on the plains, the midpoint between the ups and downs. In a word, most of life is routine. We should be thankful for this since everyday routines are amazing opportunities. Routine life gives us opportunities that change eternity.

The word *routine* is related to the word *route*. It comes from a Latin word that essentially means "a beaten path." This is a great way to describe much of our lives: washing dishes, accomplishing tasks at work, picking up toys, mowing the lawn, making dinner, attending community events, changing diapers, reading to kids at bedtime, paying bills, and so on.

But what is routine and ordinary from an earthly perspective is in reality jam-packed with opportunities to change eternity. In truth, most of our opportunity to live a dynamic, vibrant Christianity will be found in what we consider "ordinary."

"It is ingrained in us that we have to do exceptional things for God—but we do not," wrote Oswald Chambers. "We have to be exceptional in the ordinary things of life and holy on the ordinary streets, among ordinary people—and this is not learned in five minutes."[5] This is exactly what the apostle Paul was getting at when he wrote: "And whatever you do, do it heartily, as to the Lord and not to men, knowing that from the Lord you will receive the reward of the inheritance; for you serve the Lord Christ" (Col. 3:23–24). For those hearty saints willing to perform everyday tasks "to the Lord," there is stored up "the reward of the inheritance." Jesus wants to heap great reward on faithfulness in the "whatever" category of our lives.

When you stop to think about it, you realize that "whatever you do" primarily refers to daily, routine tasks. Special crowns will be given and special places of leadership in the joy of the Master will be assigned as a result of these "ordinary" involvements (see Matthew 25:21). All this, just for faithfulness in performing temporal, earthly tasks.

You may ask, "Do you really expect me to treat changing a dirty diaper or writing an office memo as something I can do for the Lord that can result in the greatest of rewards for me?" In a word, yes. If you're willing to adopt the Bible's perspective and choose to look above the circumstances, then little things are very big things. When Paul wrote to the Colossian saints, they were just regular folks. Some of them, in fact, were household slaves (see Colossians 3:22). And what was their ministry that it should reap such great reward? Plowing fields, feeding cattle, sweeping floors, cleaning bathrooms, preparing meals. And completing their tasks to the best of their ability with an eye toward God's approval. Apparently God values the routine far more than we tend to.

"Therefore, whether you eat or drink, or whatever you do, do all to the glory of God" (1 Cor.10:31). Once again, ". . . whatever you do" includes, for the most part, routine activities. What's more common, more routine, more overwhelmingly ordinary than eating or drinking? And that's why I believe Paul chose these two things to illustrate God's intense interest in every area of our lives.

For the believer, every area of life—from brushing one's teeth to planting a garden to making love to one's spouse to changing the car's oil—is spiritual. Period. No exceptions. There simply is no "common" task when we adopt the Bible's perspective. For every one of God's children there is an exhilarating purpose and a radical richness wrapped inside every routine activity—if we have the eyes to see it.

So what's the secret to joy in the daily routine of life?

A Job Well Done Makes God Smile

Work matters, but why? It's not about the money, earthly recognition, or even one's personal satisfaction, though all these have their place. The most important thing about doing a great job is what God thinks about it. God loves it when we excel. It makes Him happy, and He wants to reward us. It also affects His reputation.

Paul wrote to Titus about this very thing. "Exhort bondservants to be obedient to their own masters, to be well pleasing in all things, not answering back, not pilfering, but showing all good fidelity, that they may adorn the doctrine of God our Savior in all things" (Titus 2:9–10). The word Paul uses for *adorn* is the same word from which we get the English word *cosmetics*. Eugene Peterson captured this imagery beautifully in his rendering of the Bible, published as *The Message*. "Then their good character will shine through their actions, adding luster to the teaching of our Savior God" (Titus 2:10, MSG).

Is work simply an unavoidable necessity? No. A thousand times, no! The dullest thing in the world is to have nothing to do. Watch children at play and notice how often they're pretending to work; that's what God wired us to do. One of the first things God did after He created Adam was give him a job. Our job is to live in an arena filled with riveted angelic spectators. Your life—just like mine—is an individualized showcase for fulfilling what God designed us to do through our own well-done handiwork, when we excel in the routine tasks of life just because God wants us to.

Once again our perspective is limited. In order to choose a true perspective, we must ground it in what God tells us. Our greatest fulfillment comes from pleasing our Creator, and He tells us explicitly what pleases Him: excelling in the routine and believing our Master will make it worth our while in due time. Remember, our first encounter with God in the Bible is that of the Master Craftsman and Creator hard at work. He hovers; He divides; He makes; He places; He creates; and more. And when the dust clears we have a universe that exceeds anything we could have dreamed in our wildest imaginations.

Consider His final assessment of all that He shaped and created. It is good. It is actually *very* good. "Then God saw everything that He had made, and indeed it was very good" (Gen. 1:31). Not surprisingly then, when the Creator Son of God becomes human, He's known by the people of his time for His excellence. "And they were astonished beyond measure, saying, 'He has done all things well...'" (Mark 7:37). On Earth, Jesus spent six times longer working as a carpenter than teaching as a rabbi. Yet the entire time He was completely doing His Father's business. I wonder how many tables He made, how many ploughs He fixed, how many chairs His rough hands hammered.

At age thirty, when He began His earthly ministry, the first words He heard from His Father were "You are My beloved Son, in You I am well pleased" (Luke 3:22). This was the Father's stamp of approval on the first thirty years of Jesus' life—years spent mostly in a dusty workshop in Galilee. They were three decades during which "Jesus increased in wisdom and stature, and in favor with God and man" (Luke 2:52). Years in which He gave to every project the best He had to offer.

The excellence we devote to every aspect of our work—even when it appears to be mundane—is a crucial way we are most like Jesus. Actually, we are like Jesus *especially* in the mundane. Dorothy Sayers, in a tremendous article titled "Why Work?" wrote this: "The church's approach to an intelligent carpenter is usually confined to exhorting him not to be drunk and disorderly in his leisure hours, and to come to church on Sundays. What the church should be telling him is this: that the very first demand that his religion makes upon him is that he should make good tables." She continued: ". . . [W]hat use is all that if in the very center of his life and occupation he is insulting God with bad carpentry?

No crooked table legs or ill-fitting drawers ever, I dare swear, came out of the carpenter's shop at Nazareth. Nor, if they did, could anyone believe that they were made by the same hand that made Heaven and earth."

Sayers made the point that the secular vocation also is a sacred one. She declared: "[A] building must be good architecture before it can be a good church; [a] painting must be well-painted before it can be a good sacred picture; [work] must be good work before it can call itself God's work."[6]

In the same article, Sayers explains that when we pull apart sacred from secular we are (in her words) "astonished to find that, as a result, the secular work of the world is turned to purely selfish and destructive ends and that the greater part of the world's intelligent workers have become irreligious, or at least, uninterested in religion." Her point, of course, is that it shouldn't surprise us at all. "How can anyone remain interested in a religion that seems to have no concern with nine-tenths of his life?" she asked. "It is the business of the church to recognize that the secular vocation, as such, is sacred. Christian people, and particularly perhaps the Christian clergy, must get it firmly into their heads that when a man or woman is called to a particular job of secular work, that is as true a vocation as though he or she were called to specifically religious work."[7]

For many of us, a huge part of our earthly life is spent in the workplace. Fortunately God doesn't see our time there as "secular."

"The maid who sweeps her kitchen is doing the will of God just as much as the monk who prays—not because she may sing a Christian hymn as she sweeps but because God loves clean floors," wrote Martin Luther. "The Christian shoemaker does his Christian duty not by putting little crosses on the shoes, but by making good shoes, because God is interested in good craftsmanship."[8]

If God's people could see everything they do as working for God, their lives would immediately be vibrant, their influence electric. Moreover, choosing this perspective gets rid of perfectionism and fear of failure because it focuses on what we can control (such as the choices we make), rather than what we cannot control (such as outcomes or results). Top-tier athletes learn to focus all their attention on what they can control—their actions. They learn that if they divert their attention to worrying about the outcome, their performance will suffer. This perspective actually gives athletes, and all of us for that matter, a better chance to gain the desired results. But irrespective of the results, God promises that if we make good choices He will reward us greatly.

God's relentless, preeminent purpose for what we become in our lives is that ". . . we be conformed to the image of His Son" (Rom. 8:29). The unseen, usually unheralded, accomplishment of common tasks provides outstanding opportunity for this very thing to come about. "So the incidents of daily life may be commonplace in the extreme," wrote British pastor F. B. Meyer, "but on them as the material foundation we may build the unseen but everlasting fabric of a noble and beautiful character."[9] No act of building a table, changing a diaper, making a sales call, picking up toys, mowing the lawn, making dinner, carpooling kids, filling out an expense report, or preparing for a meeting is ever wasted if it is done in a manner that pleases God.

Big Things Are Determined by Small Things

We learned from Job that circumstances in the valley are a means rather than an end. The same is true of circumstances on the plains: they are simply the terrain of a journey taken one step at a time. One step may be viewed as a very small thing, but second steps can only follow first steps. The perspective of the plains involves seeing our circumstances as the terrain of our journey and every step as an important move toward what God wants for us. With this perspective, no circumstance is insignificant.

In Scripture winning at life means winning in the way God defines winning. "Do you not know that those who run in a race all run, but one receives the prize? Run in such a way that you may obtain it. And everyone who competes for the prize is temperate in all things. Now they do it to obtain a perishable crown, but we for an imperishable crown" (1 Cor. 9:24–25).

In ancient times just as today, Olympic athletes had to diligently train and carefully avoid whatever would cause them to be disqualified. Nothing is more mundane than the daily grind of training.

Rising early in the morning, repeating the same exercises over and over and over again, carefully monitoring what one eats, and then doing it all again. But ultimately the sum total of all the small things—when they are done with excellence— leads to the big thing of winning.

In the Greek system of Olympic games, you were only eligible to compete if you were born a Greek. Likewise, the starting point for becoming a citizen of God's "nation" is to be "born of God" by trusting Christ as our Savior. At that moment we're given a new nature, baptized by the Holy Spirit into the death and resurrection of Jesus, and made partakers of His divine nature. Birth is something we can't lose, whether we're talking about physical birth or spiritual.

But being born into life is merely a prerequisite to winning at life. Becoming a champion requires crossing the finish line. In Greek Olympic training, you could be disqualified if you slacked off and didn't try your best. Athletes had to take meticulous care of the many, many small things to achieve final victory. In 1 Corinthians 9, Paul applied this analogy to himself. The context is Paul defending against criticism from competing authorities who claimed Paul was not a *real* apostle because he worked to earn his own way. Paul replied that he had every right to earn a living from the gospel, but instead he had chosen not to. Why? Because he didn't want to do anything, no matter how small, that might be lead to him abusing his authority, and in doing so disqualify himself from gaining from Christ the greatest of rewards.

Paul said it this way, "What is my reward then? That when I preach the gospel, I may present the gospel of Christ without charge, that I may not abuse my authority in the gospel" (1 Cor. 9:18). Paul then follows this with this analogy of winning the Greek Olympics and adds his perspective about the need for daily discipline in the small things of life in order to stay in the race.

> "Do you not know that those who run in a race all run, but one receives the prize? Run in such a way that you may obtain it. And everyone who competes for the prize is temperate in all things. Now they do it to obtain a perishable crown, but we for an

imperishable crown. Therefore I run thus: not with uncertainty. Thus I fight: not as one who beats the air. But I discipline my body and bring in in to subjection, lest when I have preached to others, I myself should become *disqualified*" (1 Cor. 9:24–27, emphasis added).

This is incredibly insightful. Paul knew himself well, and he apparently realized he was prone to abuse authority. We see that in the book of Acts prior to Saul's (Paul's) meeting Jesus on the road to Damascus. At the time the Pharisee Saul had been abusing his authority by persecuting fellow Jews who had believed in Jesus. Although Paul was transformed by Jesus, he still realized this negative tendency about his base nature. But Paul wanted to win at life. He was competitive, and he wanted to win the prize from Jesus for living faithfully. Paul did not want to do anything that would disqualify him from receiving the prize.

So he disciplined himself by earning his own way, by working a trade, to reduce the risk that he might become a hypocrite by not living out the gospel in everything he did. Paul described this struggle as being similar to a boxing match, which required him to discipline his own flesh. He wanted to win, and setting aside the comfort of receiving financial support in ministry gave him a better chance to win. So for Paul, one of the greatest saints in the Bible, the road to winning in his life was paved with the everyday, mundane, repetitive task of earning a living. Paul saw his life on the plains brimming with opportunity.

In the same way, winning the Great Prize of Life (God's reward for the way we live after our new birth) consists of similarly small steps, a myriad of them. Each step should be intentionally chosen from a true perspective. The difference is that in life, we're not racing against other humans. Rather, we're competing against ourselves, like a cross-country runner working to achieve a personal best time. When you win at life, you'll hear from God: "Well done, good and faithful servant" (see Matthew 25:23). That praise will make the greatest earthly rewards seem by comparison like the forgotten youth-soccer trophies stored in the attic.

One example Jesus often uses is the act of giving a "cup of cold water in my name" (Matt. 10:42). If you visit Israel, you'll see this was a more difficult task than you'd think. In Jesus' time, in order to get a cup of cold water one would have to descend perhaps a hundred steps into a cistern to reach the water level. Then the person would draw water, hike back up the steps, and pour the water. It's a task most people could carry out, but it involved considerable trouble. That's why Jesus used this example. It doesn't matter how gifted we are. What matters supremely is our willingness to do the (often annoying) little things "in His Name."

As we focus on small things, we shake the foundations of this present world. "A cup of cold water in my Name" is a word picture for any event, action, or sacrifice that focuses on doing what God asks of us. We do these things to please Him. Whether it be with our children, in our homes, our communities, our neighborhoods, our jobs, our investments, or our churches, even the smallest, unseen acts of faithfulness are headline news in heaven. Helen Keller put it well: "I long to accomplish a great and noble task, but it is my chief duty to accomplish small tasks as if they were great and noble."[10]

We Are Judged by What We Do with What We Have

It would make no sense for us to be judged by what we would do if we had something other than what we have. Rather, we are judged by what we actually do with what we have been given.

Perhapst you've heard the old story about a farmer talking to a preacher.

Preacher: Farmer Brown, if you had fifty cows would you give fifteen of them to the Lord's work?

F.B.: Preacher, you know if I had fifty cows I would give fifteen to the Lord's work.

Preacher: Farmer Brown, if you had thirty cows, would you give ten to the Lord's work?

F.B.: Preacher, you know if I had thirty cows I would give ten to the Lord's work.

Preacher: Farmer Brown, if you had twenty cows, would you give five to the Lord's work?

F.B.: Aw, come on Preacher. You know I have twenty cows!

Not a great joke, but it makes an important point. Our calling is not to forecast what we would do if we had more. Instead, we are called to make full use, and the best use, of what we have at any given time. "For if there is first a willing mind, it is accepted according to what one has, and not according to what he does not have" (2 Cor. 8:12).

Jesus taught that to whom much is given, much is expected (see Luke 12:48). This does, of course, imply that to whom little is given, little is expected. But never did Jesus say, under any circumstance, that *nothing* is expected. The Gospels are filled with the reality that Jesus' judgment will be based on heart attitude and personal willingness, rather than what this world tends to esteem as successful accomplishment.

"And He looked up and saw the rich putting their gifts into the treasury, and He saw also a certain poor widow putting in two mites," Luke wrote (21:1–4). "So He said, 'Truly I say to you that this poor widow has put in more than all; for all these out of their abundance have put in offerings for God, but she out of her poverty put in all the livelihood that she had.'"

The poor widow didn't sit around forecasting what she *would* give if she just had more money. She just rained down every drop God had entrusted into her care. The widow's perspective is important today as an antidote to materialism and greed. Compelled by her love for God and desire to please Him, the widow gave beyond what would've been considered prudent. Unlike the Pharisees, she didn't look around to see who was watching. And unlike the wealthy, she didn't give out of a surplus of riches, which would have left plenty for her own use. She just gave out of what had been entrusted to her. She wasn't even aware of the ramifications of her quiet, humble obedience. Her gift of two mites (think of a current-day penny) may not have seemed like much to the temple crowd that day. But our Lord saw it differently. From that day forward, this unnamed, obscure widow would become an example *par excellence* of the kind of giving that catches our Lord's attention.

We should "rain" when we make offerings to God in every facet of life. As with the Colossians passage that admonishes us to do "whatever we do" as unto the Lord, Jesus' praise of the widow applies to "whatever you do" (Col. 3:23–24). This perspective shows that each one of us is rich beyond measure when we're rich toward God in small, everyday opportunities.

If you're at all like me, you grew up being guilted into giving money to churches or perhaps to other worthy causes. I got the impression that my secular occupation was important only to the degree it provided money I could give to "official Christians," meaning full-time, salaried ministry staff. But this interpretation doesn't hold water. I started studying the Bible to determine what God wants of me when it comes to giving. The parable of the widow raises an important question: does God expect us to give *all* we have? The unequivocal answer is "Yes."

When you think about everything you have, consider that *it all belongs to God*. And paradoxically, God gives us "all things richly to enjoy" (1 Tim. 6:17). How do we make sense of these seemingly contradictory statements? Here's what I've come up with: we should hold all things as stewards on behalf of God, and we should be willing at any time to use whatever we possess in whatever way God directs. That includes transferring money or earthly ownership of prized possessions to someone else's stewardship if God leads. We should consider all we possess as something to invest, to enjoy, or to use to serve others to advance God's work on Earth.

I'm in a business that constantly makes investments; in fact, every well we drill is a new investment. We're always building and have multiple companies. It's a little like farming, where you constantly plant, watch the crops grow, then harvest. When I give money to something "charitable" (which might include doing something through an organization or personally), I still view it as an investment. When you make a monetary investment, you hope you'll get a return within a matter of years. With a charitable "investment," there is no monetary payback, but if given with the right heart, it comes with a promised return guaranteed by God in the life to come. It's like a savings account for the next life.

We traveled to Ireland for David's wedding, and while we were there we visited Ireland's national archeological museum. On display were a large number of artifacts taken from ancient graves. (Isn't it interesting that we consider it horrible to rob someone's grave from our era, but perfectly fine to rob a grave from a past era?) It was common practice for people to place a loved one's favorite possessions in his or her grave, hoping the person could have use of the possessions in the next life. Obviously that didn't work. But there *is* a way to make it work: invest in people now in a way that can't be paid back. God promises *He* will pay us back.

It's common for people of financial means to have an investment portfolio that includes safe investments, which ensure you'll have money available even if things go awry, along with higher-risk investments, which allow your savings to grow over time. I do both and also include in my investment portfolio a third category—"eternal" investments.

The safest financial investment is one guaranteed by the United States government. It also pays the lowest interest rate. As I write this, a thirty-year U.S. Treasury bill is paying a little less than 3 percent. But God has promised a "hundredfold" return for any money we forego for His sake (see Mark 4:20). I don't know what "hundredfold" means mathematically. But a thirty-year investment at 3 percent will pay you about two-and-a-half times your initial investment. That isn't bad. But compared to something guaranteed by God, where you get one-hundred times your money back . . . That's like earning a 17 percent, risk-free return. In the physical world, that's unheard of. And it might mean that you get a 100 percent interest rate, which would mean after thirty years you would receive a billion times your initial investment.

I suspect that what God is trying to get across is that small charitable investments made in this life will pay back in ways we can't really fathom. This is precisely why Jesus used the cup-of-cold-water analogy. You might not be able to afford the cost of building a new wing for a hospital, but you can offer a cup of cold water in His name.

Just as dividing work from your life of faith is a false distinction, so is dividing what's yours from what's God's. Everything we have is passing through our hands on its way to someone else. It's our privilege to be stewards of these gifts for a time. When we adopt this perspective of stewardship, the fear of loss and the pressure to gain more no longer have a place.

Excellence of Work Can Open Opportunities of Influence

I am by nature a tightwad. My mom once told me that when I was a boy the ladies at church would hold me upside down to get a nickel offering out of my pocket. When I got older, if I was having lunch with a friend or colleague, I'd have "alligator arms" when it came time to pick up the check. That changed after I understood the parable of the unrighteous steward.

Jesus told His disciples about a scoundrel who was discovered pilfering his master's fortune (see Luke 16:1-13). The master warned the steward that he would be audited, so the steward devised a plan to stay out of poverty without having to beg or do heavy labor. (He claimed he was too weak to work.) The scoundrel made the rounds and started forgiving debts that were owed to his master. Why? He was looking ahead to the day he would be fired. By forgiving debts now, he was counting on those whose debts he forgave receiving him into their homes once he was fired. Jesus commended the scoundrel—not for his morals, but for his shrewdness.

Jesus used this parable to admonish His disciples to copy the scoundrel's shrewdness. Jesus criticized His disciples for not understanding what the people of the world understand and practice: the principle of reciprocity. You scratch my back, I'll scratch yours. One hand washes the other. This is the way business still operates all these years later.

Jesus said His followers should do likewise, but for a greater purpose, and in the spiritual realm. Jesus exhorted His disciples to learn the parable's lesson, "And I tell you, make friends for yourselves by how you use worldly wealth, so that when it runs out you will be *welcomed into the eternal homes"* (Luke 16:9, emphasis added).

God is the Master in the parable, of course. And He's telling us to pilfer *His money* and then use it to bless others. In turn they will invite us to their parties in the next life, in the New Earth. So we benefit in the same way as the scoundrel, but in the next life, and God is happy with that. Of course, all money is God's money. After I understood this lesson, I started grabbing the check whenever someone would let me. *This is not my money,* I now think. *But I get to use it to bless people, and that makes my Master happy. Plus I'm going to get on invitation lists to some awesome homes!* I try to be shrewd as Jesus instructs.

Most of us see influence as related to holding a position of power (positional), and therefore we feel it's unattainable. As I discovered firsthand, however, positional influence is actually a weak form of power. An approach based on "Do what I say, not what I do" doesn't generate lasting influence. In contrast, influence based on respect— referred to as "referent power"—is vastly superior. When people see you consistently live out your values, they want to follow your example. This biblical perspective revolutionizes our view of what makes a person important or influential. I had to go through my first "Job experience" to understand this reality.

King Solomon, a man known for wisdom, wrote: "Do you see a man who excels in his work?

He will stand before kings; He will not stand before unknown men" (Prov. 22:29). We should do our work well for many reasons, but one reason is the unique sphere of influence it might allow us to have. We never know what doors may open, but it's not ours to know. We just trust. "And whatever you do, do it heartily, as to the Lord and not to men . . ." (Col. 3:23). And leave it in God's hands to open whatever doors He wants. These are often stunning, surprising doors.

So much of our everyday lives does not take place on the mountaintops or in the valleys. Our lives are spent on the unheralded plains. These plains—the endless routines of life—can be embraced rather than just endured, but only if we maintain the right perspective on their significance. By looking above the circumstances, we see that the plains of everyday life are full of eternal adventure. Faithfulness in the small things of life is a big part of what makes our "routine" lives epic.

I learned a lot from reading the words of Brother Lawrence, a kitchen helper in a French monastery in the 1600s who decided to "practice the presence of God" while carrying out ordinary kitchen tasks. One man who talked to him described Brother Lawrence's methods for approaching God. Brother Lawrence did routine chores, what he termed common business, "...without any view of pleasing people, and – as far we are capable -purely for the love of God." He also said when his times of scheduled prayer were finished, nothing changed for him, "...because he still continued with God, praising and blessing Him with all his might.""[11] Brother Lawrence left an enormous spiritual legacy simply from a life lived performing kitchen tasks with a grateful attitude in communion with God. When I can pull off a perspective such as his, it helps me see reality as it truly is.

Martin Luther King Jr. spoke to students on October 26, 1967. He told them: "Don't just set out to do a good job. Set out to do such a good job that the living, the dead, or the unborn couldn't do it any better. If it falls your lot to be a street sweeper, sweep streets like Michelangelo painted pictures, sweep streets like Beethoven composed music, sweep streets like Leontyne Price sings before the Metropolitan Opera. Sweep streets like

Shakespeare wrote poetry. Sweep streets so well that all the hosts of heaven and earth will have to pause and say: here lived a great street sweeper who swept his job well."[12]

The true perspective is that God considers every task we take on to be great if we do it to please Him. When we adopt the true perspective, every second of every day overflows with value and purpose. We can take great joy and live in thanksgiving for the amazing, one-time opportunity we are given to know God by faith during the surprisingly short time we have on Earth.

Now we turn to one of the most dangerous challenges we'll face in our epic, two-minute journey—prosperity.

5

PERSPECTIVE ON THE MOUNTAINTOP

Any form of prosperity—fame, riches, or status—can sidetrack us like few other developments in life. In many ways the mountaintop of prosperity is more dangerous than the valley or the plains. The mountaintop can lull its victims into spiritual lethargy while convincing them they're winning at the game of life. And, alas, the mountaintop experience will ultimately disappoint, for experiences are, of themselves, never enough to satisfy the hunger in our souls. We saw a small illustration of this through a song.

"Today Is Beautiful" was the first of our son David's songs that played on the radio. Our entire family experienced a moment similar to a scene in the movie *That Thing You Do*. In the movie a fledgling band, The Oneders (sounds like *wonders*), suddenly had a radio hit. And in our car—just like in the movie—everyone was screaming with excitement the first time we heard David's song on the car radio. Seeing "David Dunn: Today Is Beautiful" on the digital display was a mountaintop experience.

His song did incredibly well, so well that it seemed destined to hit No. 1. But alas, it was knocked off-course by a poor focus-group result that caused it to be pulled from the frequent-play rotation.

And so it is with mountaintop experiences. The first time we heard the song on the radio, it was exhilarating. Then it became routine. Then it led to disappointment because it didn't make No. 1. Mountaintops can turn into plains and then into valleys. What we lose sight of is that mountaintops pose a particular hazard, the propensity to lose a true perspective, which can lead to great ruin. Interestingly the lyrics of "Today is Beautiful" are about choosing a true perspective and were inspired by an episode that occurred between two of our grandkids while our entire family visited a Disney theme park.

As you know, one of the Disney taglines is "the happiest place on Earth." On this day, however, my grandson Brady had a monumental meltdown because his sister Addie would not let him push the empty stroller. It's easy to say to the child *"Don't you realize where you are? You're in Disney*land*!* Focus on all the happiness around you." But we adults do the same thing, but in an adult way.

This moment inspired David to write the lyrics to "Today Is Beautiful." David explained, "*Just look around* you *and realize pushing the stroller is insignificant.* We, as humanity, do the same thing when we're going on about our lives and some little problem comes up. It irks us, and we focus on it so much that it becomes this huge ordeal that puts us in a state of misery that we can't get over.

"We neglect to just lift our eyes and see that, in reality, we are living in Disneyland. We are in this place where we have a God who loves and cares about us and wants the best for us. If we can view that problem from His point of view, from an outside perspective, we can see it for what it is— just a stroller that our older sister won't let us push. It might even be an opportunity for growth."

In other words, most of life is a Disneyland opportunity if we can maintain the correct perspective regarding daily difficulties. "But if you lift your eyes, see it in a different light," David wrote in his song. "Just a cloud up in the open sky. Let the rain fall away, for today is beautiful."[13]

Sadly, the bumper sticker "He who dies with the most toys wins" aptly describes a life of accumulating empty strollers to push while we miss the best that Disneyland has to offer. Most of us have fallen into a trap of living with a materialistic perspective, similar to my grandson Brady when he wanted more than anything to push an empty stroller. We go to Disneyland, but we focus on the stroller instead of the amazing rides all around us.

While Moriah's passing was much more devastating than just a passing cloud, "Today Is Beautiful" was the theme of her yellow-balloon memorial service. It was fitting. Our primary challenge was to choose a true perspective through the grief.

This doesn't mean we shouldn't enjoy hearing our son's song played on the radio or seeing him appear on *The Voice*. Paul wrote to his protégé

Timothy: "Command those who are rich in this present age not to be haughty, nor to trust in uncertain riches but in the living God, who gives us richly all things to enjoy" (1 Tim. 6:17). God made *all things* for us to enjoy. We are to savor and enjoy our good moments but without trusting in them. We are not to make the tragic mistake of believing that mountaintop circumstances are the path to fulfillment. That's what I think Paul meant when he wrote: ". . . nor to trust in uncertain riches . . ." Remember, there are only three things we control, and one of them is whom (or, in this case, what) we trust. God gives a stern warning about the danger of trusting in mountaintop circumstances such as riches. Riches are fleeting; only God is certain.

The very best mountaintop circumstance can never bring lasting fulfillment, just as money can't buy happiness. As we saw with Job, the greatest opportunity in this life is to know God by faith. That is as true on the mountaintop as it is on the plains as it is in the valley. On the mountaintop, however, God often is harder to see. On the mountaintop we can more easily choose a false perspective, believing we actually do control our circumstances and that they will fulfill us. We tend to seek God only when circumstances bring us to a point of despairing in all else.

It does not have to be that way. If we choose a true perspective, we can enjoy the mountaintop experiences fully and unreservedly, and still come to know God by faith every step along the way. Yes, even when resting on a summit.

Let's look at four common types of mountaintop prosperity offered by our materialistic, stroller-envying world.

The Potential Danger of Stuff

"[L]et not the rich man glory in his riches . . ." (Jer. 9:23).

As a kid, not only was I stingy, but I had the wrong perspective on success. I harbored the ambition to be a professional athlete, a professional musician, and a company president. I believed accomplishing one of those things would bring me happiness. Though I didn't have the aptitude or the required commitment to become either a professional athlete or musician, I did have an aptitude for business. Recently I was awarded "CEO of the Year" for large independent oil and gas companies, and God has blessed me with a level of material success beyond anything I could have imagined.

I'm grateful to God for this success, but I've also learned to be grateful for the ditches I fell into along the way (including my initial self-imposed "Job experience"), as well as the small, everyday things of life such as clouds and sunsets. If given the choice, I always would choose easy, pleasant circumstances. However, I no longer equate easy circumstances with happiness. I know that's not a true perspective.

I've also discovered firsthand what seems a common discovery when someone achieves a dream: it's not as fulfilling as you'd expected. I have learned firsthand that what the world tells us will deliver true happiness simply won't. If we're paying attention, we all eventually discover we have a thirst no worldly experience can quench. So no matter what the world might promise, we know ahead of time that the promise is empty.

"I think everybody should get rich and famous and do everything they ever dreamed of," wrote actor Jim Carrey, "so they can see that it's not the answer."[14]

We all spend time trying to get wealthy, but God tells us how we can be rich *now*. "Buy gold from me," Jesus says in Revelation 3:18. How in the world do we buy gold from God? The Bible's answer may initially seem strange: we gain great riches from God by listening to Him. When He knocks on the door of our heart and asks to come in, invite Him in for dinner (see Revelation 3:20). It has sometimes taken a two-by-four of unwelcome circumstances to get me to listen, but I think I have listened . . . at least a little. I've learned to see negative circumstances as a great gift that can lead to the abundant riches that become available by simply listening to God.

What true riches I have stem directly from listening to God. Biblical wisdom exposes our idea of earthly wealth for the fool's gold it really is. God's transcendent wisdom and instruction lead us to choose a right perspective.

I haven't always viewed the Bible as a mine full of jewels of wisdom waiting for me to dig them up. Growing up in church, I came to view the Bible as mostly bad news. I saw it as a book of obligation and condemnation. Although it offered a great rescue to come at the end of one's life, the rest of it was not all that pleasant. I didn't think of it as a gift from God or a treasure map to great riches.

But later on I saw that listening to the Bible's wisdom is the same as "buying gold." I stopped reading the Bible with fear and stopped worrying about condemnation. Instead I began to enjoy the Bible. I realized God doesn't just love me, He *likes* me and really wants me to succeed. That's why He puts hard things in my path—so I can learn. The Bible has become the primary way I find reality and a true perspective. So as I share the Bible passages in this book, I feel like I'm letting you see my treasure map.

God's Idea of True Riches

Listening to the wisdom God offers from His Word provides a view of eternity that transforms every minute of every day into an opportunity to acquire a lasting treasure. This is the only treasure that can dramatically exceed the wildest dreams of any earthly quest for gold. The Bible promises that we can obtain an imperishable spiritual treasure that never can be taken from us.

Contrast this with the world's notion of riches, which is based on acquiring things we want but don't have. If we believe we can't be happy unless we gain more than we have, then we will never enjoy our current circumstances—what we *do* have. But if we listen to God and adopt a true perspective, we can enjoy our present circumstances and even enjoy striving, regardless of the outcome. Without this, you and I will never adopt a perspective that embraces struggle and gains fulfillment from the epic adventure of life.

The world says happiness comes from getting a better job, a bigger house, outstanding children, better treatment from one's spouse, or a prestigious award as top producer, or the fastest rising star in one's field of endeavor. But this thinking is ultimately bankrupt. Happiness that's grounded in acquiring what we don't have will never allow us to enjoy what we do have. Adopting the world's perspective is embracing a life filled with the futility that accompanies spiritual poverty.

For many years I have tried to choose a true perspective, and it's still a daily struggle. Choosing a true perspective in a deceptive world requires diligence, and I still mess up often. This is part of the reason why the Bible likens a Christian walk to training for an Olympic race. It takes knowledge and daily practice to learn to see life through the lens of faith.

But make no mistake. Choosing a right, biblical perspective is not what's commonly referred to as "positive thinking." Positive thinking, in essence, boils down to a belief that you can control circumstances by how you think. This, of course, is silly. Truth often reveals things we'd rather not see (such as realizing our view of our self is inflated). However, the most positive thing we can do is to see reality for what it is, even when the truth hurts. Only a true perspective provides a sufficient foundation and leads to lasting fulfillment. As I have shifted my perspective—focusing more on how this life is an incredible, one-time opportunity to prepare by faith for eternity—my fulfillment has increased. By embracing the Bible's exhortation that happiness stems from service, even to the point of sacrifice, I've found true fulfillment that's only a down payment on eternal riches. Suffering for serving in faith is something angels can't experience, although they long to understand it.

Viewing life through this lens is transformational in our epic adventure. The secret to fulfilling our longing to be someone important is to simply receive it. As it turns out, happiness, ambition, and heroic accomplishment all are byproducts of living a life of faithful and courageous service wherever God places us. But we first have to deliberately adopt a true perspective that enables us to transcend what's visible in this present world.

Don't Be Enticed by Stuff

Many people's lives are frantically driven by the deep-seated belief that the best life has to offer is found in owning a lot of stuff. Sounds very unsophisticated when it's put like this, doesn't it? Whether it be large amounts of cash, stock certificates, twenty-four-carat diamonds, million-dollar homes, Rolex watches, Gucci handbags, Armani suits, Rolls Royces, or everyday Walmart specials, it's all just stuff. It was stuff a hundred years ago; it is stuff today when it is new and impressive looking; and it will be stuff a hundred years from now when it's decaying in a landfill. Not that there is anything inherently wrong with material goods. Nor is there anything wrong with working diligently toward acquiring things. The danger lies in what we believe stuff can do for us. Our Lord warned us when He said, "Take heed and beware of covetousness, for one's life does not consist in the abundance of the things he possesses" (Luke 12:15).

First, stuff never does for the soul what it boldly promises. You and I know it never delivers deep satisfaction. As Solomon wrote, "He who loves silver will not be satisfied with silver; nor he who loves abundance, with increase. This also is vanity" (Ecc. 5:10). Whenever there's a gain in wealth, there also is a corresponding gain in appetite for more. It's human nature.

This tendency surfaces in matters that go far beyond money or material possessions. We were exhilarated the first time we heard our son's song on the radio. Before we knew it, we looked forward to the day when his song would reach No. 1 on the hit charts. The truth is, however, we can never win at life through always wanting more. Wealth in any realm of life, once it's acquired, always leads to a new level of desire for more wealth. John Rockefeller was asked how much money it took to make a man happy. His immediate answer was "A little more."

The worldly philosophy of materialism causes us to undervalue what we do have and esteem what we don't. But if we adopt God's perspective, we can "richly enjoy" everything we do have. Instead of spending every day of our earthly life wishing we were enjoying even greater financial wealth, we can thoroughly enjoy the epic life God designed especially for us.

Second, stuff can't provide lasting significance. All the wealth a person acquires on Earth is immediately forfeited at the instant of death. Following the funeral of a very wealthy man, one of his friends said to another, "Just how much do you think John left behind?" The friend rightly responded, "Everything." Though you can't take your stuff with you, this does not negate the importance of diligence, hard work, and the sweat-soaked pursuit of excellence. In fact, God commands it. Laziness is not the antidote to materialism.

By refusing the siren call of wealth, we can come to know God by faith, continuing to walk in dependence on Him even when the world would tell us it's unnecessary. William James was right when he said, "The greatest use of life is to spend it for something that will outlast it."[15] As our Lord put it, "Do not labor for the food which perishes, but for the food which endures to everlasting life . . ." (John 6:27). The true perspective is that we are just stewards of the stuff; it's passing through our hands on the way to someone else.

True happiness flows from a perspective of thanksgiving, recognizing that every moment of our life is truly an amazing gift. We can continue to walk in faith on the mountaintop, even when it seems unnecessary. As Brother Lawrence showed us, the valley is not the only place we can learn to know God by faith. We must learn to walk by faith across every type of terrain, through every circumstance. Arguably it takes more faith to live in dependence on God when every circumstance of life tells us dependence is unnecessary. Maybe this is why, in Matthew 19, Jesus described how difficult it is for rich people to enter the kingdom of God. Fortunately, Jesus also said, "With God, all things are possible" (v. 26).

Reputational Prosperity: The Danger of Prestige

"And do you seek great things for yourself?
Do not seek them . . ." (Jer. 45:5).

The word *prestige* aptly comes from a Latin root that means "to create an illusion, to trick someone." One of the greatest dangers we face is the heady wine of reputational prosperity. It's easy for prestige to trick us into believing that life is best when other people hold us in high esteem. There's nothing inherently wrong with prestige, of course. The Bible tells us eternal life comes in two ways: a) the *unconditional gift* of eternal life is freely given when we believe that Jesus died on the cross for our sins. b) but the Bible also speaks of eternal life as a *conditional reward* given to those who ". . . by patient continuance in doing good seek glory, honor, and immortality [legacy]" (Rom. 2:7).

Seeking glory, honor, and a lasting remembrance from God by being faithful even in small things is what God seeks to reward. Jesus modeled this in John 17 when He prayed to His Father to glorify Him (Jesus). Our problem is not that we seek glory and honor, it's that we crave it from the wrong source. Romans 2 shows us that God does not condone "self-seeking." But seeking honor from God is exactly what Jesus did, and it's what He invites us to do.

Be warned: it's costly. The epic tale that shapes much of Western civilization is Homer's *The Iliad*. The story's hero, Achilles, is presented a choice. He can either live a long, comfortable life and die unknown, or he can live a short and violent life fighting a great battle and be remembered forever. It's a no-brainer for Achilles: short and glorious wins out.

Achilles was willing to give his life to gain glory. But he also was a spoiled, self-seeking brat.

God invites us to be heroes in an epic adventure, to gain the glory of His great pleasure, and to leave a lasting legacy in eternity. As with the choices given to Achilles, God asks us to give our lives. But God's invitation has nothing to do with the self-seeking motivations of someone such as Achilles. Instead, God asks us to set aside self and to serve cups of cold water in His name every day. In doing this we live an epic, Achillean life—but from God's perspective. We give our lives for glory, but we are giving our lives in service to God seeking glory from Him.

The Creator of the universe wants us to be great. In fact, God placed in us a desire for greatness. But when we try to generate greatness as a way to call attention to ourselves, or when we manipulate it in others, we essentially are transformed into self-worshippers.

Ironically, egotism will rob you of yourself. That might sound a little crazy. However, when you seek fame, you inevitably become someone else in order to be liked. In the process you lose the person you really are. The result is that who you truly are, the real you, ends up with no relationships.

And that means you're all alone. The deepest joys of life include knowing others and being known. My guess is that eternal life as a reward will largely stem from coming to know God through walking by faith over the terrain of life and living above our circumstances.

The widow who gave all she had did not know anyone was watching. But Jesus saw her and today the poor widow is famous. That's just one illustration of the true fame God promises. It takes a perspective of informed faith to believe this is true, but how can you improve on a promise from the living God who desires your very best?

As usual, though, the world offers a counterfeit, fleeting, worldly fame that causes us to lose ourselves. Our son David is famous in a small way because of his music. He wrote a song called "Ready to Be Myself," which includes these lyrics:

> I'm tired of the way
> The way that I change
> I rearrange
> Myself to be
> The man that everybody loves,

So I become someone I'm not.
Who am I gonna be
When nobody's watching me?
I want to be real!
What am I gonna do
To live what I know is true?
I let go!
Oh I've been someone else
I'm ready to be myself.[16]

When we let go of the false image we think others want us to be so we can pursue excellence in being the person God made us to be, we discover the great joy of knowing and being known. As a bonus, when we walk by faith and refuse to rely on earthly prosperity, we also experience irreplaceable joy from and with God.

Reputational prosperity—using the same strategy as materialism—convinces us that happiness will come from the accolades we *don't* have. If we accept that lie, we will forfeit the enjoyment of the relationships we *do* have. A love of self can never be fully satisfied. It always is seeking out new accolades, new praises, new awards, new ways of being recognized for one's greatness.

The only way to break free from the trap of glorifying ourselves is to believe the truth that earthly prestige has very little lasting power. It fades quickly and is even more quickly forgotten. "I have seen the wicked in great power and spreading himself like a native green tree. Yet he passed away, and behold, he was no more; Indeed I sought him, but he could not be found" (Ps. 37:35–36).

I once visited the National Baseball Hall of Fame and Museum. I saw memorials to great players like Babe Ruth. But what struck me most was the fact that I'd never heard of the majority of players lionized in that baseball shrine. The knowledge of players who preceded my generation was reduced to no more than a name on a plaque. In contrast, God promises that our small things done faithfully will be remembered *forever*.

God commands us in 1 Peter 5 to humble ourselves. Along with the command He gives us the promise that He will exalt us in due time as a reward for our obedience (see v. 6). It takes great trust in God and His benevolent intent toward us to adopt this perspective. But when we seek earthly prestige, we can expect, at best, the prestige to last for a very brief time. In contrast, God promises that if we seek Him and walk in His ways, we will receive a reward of fame that lasts forever.

Intellectual Prosperity — The Potential Danger of Smarts

A high IQ is a wonderful gift, but reliance upon our own wits can be a hazardous burden to bear during our epic adventure. As with the other forms of prosperity, there is nothing inherently wrong with intellect. A bright mind is a wonderful gift from God, and it can create untold good when it's surrendered to the God who created it. But evil can also stem from gifted minds. History is filled with the accounts of intelligent people who did horrific things. In the twentieth century alone we saw Adolf Hitler and Joseph Stalin—no doubt very smart men—who put their gifts to use causing unimaginable horror. Great minds have the potential to produce great good or great damage, all depending on to whom or to what purpose the intellect is surrendered.

The Marxist philosophy of materialism, which denies all things supernatural, is arguably the spirit of the current age. Because this philosophy has become so popular, it is common practice to ignore or deny that it was the intellectual foundation underlying the murder of tens of millions who resisted the ruling Communist Party in Stalin's Russia. But an intellectual foundation of materialism inevitably leads to authoritarian intolerance.

And really, the great issue is "Whom will we choose to trust?" This is one of the three things in life that we control. Every mind is surrendered to something. In fact, every human faculty is a surrendered faculty. "And do not present your members (i.e., faculties) as instruments of unrighteousness to sin, but present yourselves to God as being alive from the dead, and your members as instruments of righteousness to God" (Rom. 6:13). Note from this passage that we ultimately have only one choice as to what we do with our mind and our other faculties. Our choice is to "present," which means "to place alongside." In other words, our choice is to surrender our faculties. But will we surrender ourselves to God or to the world and sin?

Our intellect can be surrendered to the revealed wisdom of God (the Bible) and the enlightening influence of God (the Holy Spirit), or it can be surrendered to the arrogant confidence of our own egos and the deceptive influences of other God-despising intellects in the world. As we ponder the choice to surrender, it is important to reflect that there is no third option. The notion of a "free thinker" is an illusion. Human reasoning can't even start without beginning with definitions. And definitions can't be proved (by definition, you might say.)

The smarter we are, the more likely we are to trust ourselves. Consider this incredible irony. Even when people with superior intellects acknowledge God as our Creator, they face the subtle danger of believing that all they need to do to comprehend God's truth is to devote deep thought to the subject. They run the risk of depending solely on the sharp mind God gave them. John Calvin wrote, "There is no worse screen to block out the Spirit than confidence in our own intelligence."[17]

Martin Luther wrote, "We cannot attain to the understanding of Scripture either by study or by the intellect. Your first duty is to begin by prayer. Entreat the Lord to grant you, of His great mercy, the true understanding of His Word. There is no other interpreter of the Word of God than the Author of this Word, as He Himself has said, 'They shall be all taught of God' (John 6:45)."[18]

Passengers on the two-minute ride must always maintain a healthy distrust in what their minds are capable of apart from a consistent, deliberate dependence upon God Himself. We can experience the greatest joy in life when we, like Job, see ourselves as small in the awesome presence of a mighty Creator. True riches, all the gold we want, come from listening to God, but listening requires humility. We must admit what we don't already know before we are willing to listen.

Experiential Prosperity: The Danger of Spiritual Highs

What could be wrong with pursuing as many spiritual highs as possible? The danger is very subtle. We can be seduced into making spiritual experiences our primary goal, rather than seeking deeper spiritual devotion. Our great calling is to love and follow Jesus wherever He leads, whenever He leads, however He leads. After all, God knows how to fulfill our longings infinitely better than we do. By choosing to trust and follow God wherever He leads, the spiritual highs God chooses for us will find us rather than our having to seek them. And the difference between the two approaches is astronomical.

There is a simple reason why Peter, James, and John had the colossal spiritual experience of seeing Christ transfigured. "Jesus took Peter, James, and John and led them up on a high mountain . . ." (Matt. 17:1). These three followers of Jesus had such a life-changing experience because Jesus *led them*. In other words, they stayed close to Christ.

They didn't know exactly where He was taking them, and they certainly had no idea what awaited them. All they did was faithfully take the next step until ultimately they were blindsided by an experience they could never have imagined. They weren't following after an experience but after a Savior, and that makes all the difference.

Oswald Chambers explained it by writing, "We have all experienced times of exaltation on the mountain, when we have seen things from God's perspective and have wanted to stay there. But God will never allow us to stay there."[19] Instead of being depressed by this fact, however, he encourages us to embrace it. "The true test of our spiritual life is in exhibiting the power to descend from the mountain. If we only have the power to go up, something is wrong. It is a wonderful thing to be on the mountain with God, but a person only gets there so that he may later go down and lift up the demon-possessed people in the valley (see Mark 9:14–18)."

Years later Peter would recount this once-in-a-lifetime experience. "For we did not follow cunningly devised fables when we made known to you the power and coming of our Lord Jesus Christ, but were eyewitnesses of His majesty. For He received from God the Father honor and glory when such a voice came to Him from the Excellent Glory: "This is My beloved Son, in whom I am well pleased" (2 Peter 1:16–17).

We also see God's sense of humor in this passage. Peter had begun to make plans to camp out and enjoy the mountaintop experience. "Then Peter answered and said to Jesus, 'Lord, it is good for us to be here; if You wish, let us make here three tabernacles: one for You, one for Moses, and one for Elijah'" (Matt. 17:4).

Naturally, Peter wanted to make the experience last, so he proposed building three "mountain cabins." But God wasn't interested in that. "While he [Peter] was still speaking, behold, a bright cloud overshadowed them, and suddenly a voice came out of the cloud, saying, 'This is My beloved Son, in whom I am well pleased. Hear Him!'" (Matt. 17:5). God made it clear. "Peter, now is not the time for talking and planning; now is the time for listening and following!"

We need to pay careful attention to this story and to the interchange between God and Peter. This is critical to understanding the true perspective related to mountaintop spiritual experiences. Our great calling is to listen to Him and follow Him. As I've mentioned, listening to God—hearing His voice—is how we "buy gold" from God (see Revelation 3:18–20). It's how we acquire an unlimited supply of goods without a dime (see Isaiah 55:1–2).

I can control whether I listen to God. Choosing to listen to Him leads to the greatest prosperity. It leads us to follow Him, know Him, and take one step after another as He leads us where He wants to take us. Sometimes it's up the mountain. Sometimes it's down into the valley. Most often, Jesus leads us to the plains—the routine, exceedingly common affairs of everyday living. The great issue on our two-minute ride is not the *where* of the ride but the *Who*.

As we get to know the One leading us, we can begin to leave it in His nail-scarred hands to decide how much time we need in each location: mountaintop, valley, or the plains. Most of all, by listening to God, we come to walk by faith through the wonderful, once-in-an-existence adventure we call life.

6

WHAT IS A JOB-LIKE EXPERIENCE?

While Terri and I were courting, we discussed our hopes and goals for marriage. I initially believed I didn't want to have children; there was just too much risk something bad could happen. I had a perspective that I could control circumstances and avoid difficulty. However, looking through a biblical lens allowed me to realize how dumb my perspective was. Subsequently, Terri and I decided to trust God and aim to have four children. Now, roughly forty years of marriage, six kids (we overshot the runway), and fifteen grandchildren later, I'm sincerely grateful for the biblical wisdom that showed me the way to true riches.

Think of all I would've missed if I had tried to control those circumstances.

A friend once told me he had observed that people with deep faith tended to suffer more. He reasoned that living a life with nominal faith was the sweet spot of life. It is likely his reasoning was more rationalization than analysis. But you might argue it is a possible takeaway from reading Job's story: "The attention God pays to His favorite servants results in a lot of pain, so it's best to be mediocre in God's eyes."

We can all agree that suffering stinks. Who wants to suffer? Not me. That leads to the question "How much of a life priority ought we to place on avoiding difficulty?" I think there are two important answers to this question. First, we ought to exert great effort to avoid self-imposed pain. Self-seeking is self-destructive. When we are confronted with a mistake, the Bible gives us some excellent advice: own up, confess, make it right, and learn the lesson.

That, of course, makes the pain even worse initially. It hurts to admit "I am wrong." But it lays the foundation for a foul-up to become a blessing. The Bible also tells us the reason God wrote down the stories of the Old Testament is so we can learn our lessons from the mistakes of others, and we don't have to do all the learning from our own mistakes (See 1 Corinthians 10:1–6). "Wisdom," as taught by the Bible, consists largely of following God's advice and avoiding self-inflicted pain.

But there is another category of suffering that stems from just living in a fallen world. Like the unavoidable, sudden death of a child, whose heart just stopped. If we want to avoid that kind of suffering, the cost is too great, since loving relationships are the underlying source of much of this kind of pain. Kids bring trouble, and lots of it. So does any good relationship. When you love someone, it creates potential for loss, as we experienced with Moriah. But it's only for a season. As much as it hurt, I would never give up knowing precious Moriah for twenty-two months in order to avoid the pain of losing her. I'm sure that when I get to heaven, Moriah's presence, rather than just my memories of her, will be a source of great joy.

As my personal story demonstrates, the lessons of Job apply to both categories of suffering. Both the self-inflicted pain of my first Job-like experience as well as the unavoidable loss of Moriah brought great personal pain. Whether life's difficulties are self-imposed or just dropped in our lap, the redemptive opportunity begins by choosing a true perspective.

Hopefully you have not lost your children, wealth, reputation, and health all at once like Job did. But pain is pain, and when we experience prolonged or deep pain and difficulty, we're in the boat with Job. That's why it makes sense that the Bible encourages all of us to learn from the story of Job, the story God wrote down for us first, even though our experiences will likely not be nearly as extreme. We can apply lessons gleaned from Job even to routine daily difficulties.

We have a Job-like experience any time our expectations about the way life is supposed to go are smashed, along with the resulting personal pain. Have you experienced the pain and loss following a miscarriage? The embarrassing disappointment of being fired? Have you tried out for a team in a sport you're good at but failed to make the cut? Did the person you thought you were going to marry choose someone else? Or perhaps you made a poor choice and are now living with the consequences. Job-like experiences are unique and personal. What one person finds exceedingly difficult, another might consider only a mild inconvenience. Any circumstance that brings the kind of pain or grief that interrupts your ability to function qualifies.

My first Job-like experience, owning up to being arrogant, would likely have been invisible if you'd watched it play out. My pain was mainly internal, set up by a standard I had set for myself crashing into the reality of miserable failure to live up to that expectation. Most circumstances surrounding me were good, others in my same station might have been elated. We are all different. We all have hopes and dreams, although what we hope and dream for might differ substantially. We all have expectations. And when those expectations are dashed, it brings pain.

If something in life crushes you, it's your Job-like experience. This gives you the opportunity to believe that God is rooting for you while taking you through life circumstances you never would have chosen on your own. In life's valleys you often find some of your greatest opportunities to know God by faith—the same experience angels long to understand.

When we are crushed, we tend to think life is happening to us, and we are victims without choices. If we choose that perspective, our circumstances become a prison. They define who we are and what we can do. But choosing to see our circumstances as merely the terrain of our journey enables us to know that we still choose our actions. We can make life choices based on faith. Then our experiences provide the opportunity to become all God meant us to be. To the extent we can immerse ourselves in a true perspective and listen to the actual message of the Bible, we can gain true and lasting riches. Learning to intentionally choose a true perspective has immense practical application in *any* situation.

We Expect Too Little of God

Our lives should be far more than merely functional. Job's story showed me how deeply God cared for Job, wanting him to have things he didn't even know he wanted. And God wants the same for all His children—for you and me. The fulfillment we experience from knowing God by faith, through the circumstances of life, far exceeds the fulfillment of any of our earthly desires.

C. S. Lewis hit on this point in his book *The Weight of Glory.* He wrote, "It would seem that our Lord finds our desires not too strong, but too weak. We are half-hearted creatures, fooling about with drink and sex and ambition when infinite joy is offered us, like an ignorant child who wants to go on making mud pies in a slum because he cannot imagine what is meant by the offer of a holiday at the sea. We are far too easily pleased."[20]

I'm beginning to understand what Lewis meant. Though God is not a cosmic vending machine, He is the source of all that's good. If we want the maximum benefit from life (and who doesn't?), we must make a key shift in perspective. We must learn to move from "God, give me what I want and I'll go along with what you want" to "God, you know what is best for me. I trust You to give me what I want, for you know my wants better than I and which wants are the best wants." When we adopt this perspective, we won't ask,

"Why me?" in the midst of troubling times. We'll be free to ask, "What's my opportunity here?"

God used my first Job-like experience to show me something I really wanted and how to gain it. I wanted to be a leader. I learned leadership doesn't mean being in control, it means taking responsibility. I had to learn to be willing to *listen* and to see things as they *actually are*. I found it particularly hard seeing myself as I really am. It hurt, but I'm very grateful to have learned a little bit of reality. Reality is an acquired taste, but it is our friend.

Through the valleys God showed me that knowing God by faith has infinite benefit beyond anything we might imagine. After I came to see all this, another verse came alive: "Eye has not seen, nor ear heard, nor have entered into the heart of man the things which God has prepared for those who love Him" (1 Corinthians 2:9, quoting Isaiah 64:4). Loving God means trusting that whatever comes into our lives is for our best. God promises that if we trust in this truth, the benefit we receive will be so enormous we can't really comprehend it in this life. I have come to tangibly believe that, and it has revolutionized my perspective on life. However, believing this does not make it an easy thing to do.

It should not surprise us that God did not want Job to miss out on knowing Him by faith even one teensy bit. Why else would God treat Job the way He did? God is either sadistic or He is giving the very best to His favorite follower. We find the truth in the latter option. God is looking to bless beyond comprehension every person who loves Him. This is not "I will do this for you, and in return I demand ..." Instead, this is "God, I will love you and trust that in due time the return will be more than I can imagine."

We are actually commanded to do this. "Therefore humble yourselves under the mighty hand of God, that He may exalt you in due time, casting all your care upon Him, for He cares for you" (1 Peter 5:6–7). If the arrangement were anything else—such as "I'll scratch your back if you scratch mine"—we would think we were in control. But God will shower infinite riches on us only when we learn to live in dependence on Him. In other words, to walk by faith. When we are commanded to do something, that's a signal that it doesn't come easily or naturally. I know all this is true, but it's still a daily challenge to actually live by faith, and I often stumble.

When We Ask to Be Spared Intense Suffering

It's also okay to ask to be delivered from Job-like circumstances we can't avoid. Jesus had a Job-like experience in the Garden of Gethsemane and asked His Father for deliverance. *Gethsemane* is a Hebrew word meaning "olive press," and that image provides a vivid picture of what was happening to Jesus. As He contemplated His coming sacrifice to bear the sins of the world on a Roman cross, He was crushed like an olive in a press. His great drops of sweat like blood, in the garden, call to mind the first press drips of virgin olive oil. And while He bore this enormous weight, He asked His Father for deliverance and for any other possible way (see Matthew 26:39).

If Jesus sought another way, it certainly is okay for us to do the same. But God decides, and sometimes He tells us, "No." That is what He told Jesus in the garden. Ultimately, Jesus said,

"Thy will be done" (see Matthew 26:39). Jesus acknowledged, "I know that you know best, and I will embrace whatever you give me as my best." And of course we know in hindsight all the great things that came from Jesus' obedience. This key perspective, which was modeled by Jesus, is a message we get first from the book of Job.

The Bible's wisdom can be appropriately described as instructions on how to live in a manner that avoids self-destruction. But even when we do stupid things, God promises He will turn those instances to our benefit. I can certainly attest to that.

My friend who wanted to avoid Christianity in order to avoid problems was wrong. I was wrong when I tried to avoid pain by not having children. Undoubtedly, I'm wrong on things now—God works on us as we are able. What I learned from my first (self-induced) Job-like experience became the foundation for the last half of my life.

What will the Job-like experience of Moriah's death lead to? I'm not sure. Perhaps I won't know in this life. But maybe this book is part of the answer. Regardless, it's helpful for me to remember Satan's complaint that God had built a "hedge" around Job, as well as the promise of 1 Corinthians 10:13 that God will never allow a temptation or trial into our lives that we can't handle. God makes deliberate decisions about what He allows into our lives. If we truly embrace the perspective that God wants only our best—and that He would not have any people He loves miss out on any blessings—we can rest in the gift of His peace.

Just as an athlete later thanks the coach for pushing him so he could excel and win the prize, sometimes God puts us through seemingly unreasonable circumstances, so we can learn to know Him in a way we otherwise could not. Knowing God by faith, not just knowing about Him, is a massively beneficial opportunity available to us but not to the angels. And it's available only in this life.

7

EMBRACE YOUR INNER SUPERHERO

Abraham is a biblical superhero because he is the Bible's premier example of walking by faith. However, as we consider the events of Abraham's life, I don't think any of his neighbors would have had a clue about his great faith. And if we were to read only about Abraham's *actions* I don't think we would either. We know Abraham had great faith because God tells us he had great faith. Superhero status achieved by walking in faith often is largely invisible. This makes sense, since faith is believing things we can't see.

Think for a moment how Abraham's walk of faith might have appeared to observers who did not have access to additional insight from the Bible. Abraham left his comfortable home in a lush area, traveled a long distance, and resettled in a desert region. He set off on a new adventure while he was old. We know from the Bible that this obedience won God's approval and elevated Abraham to the status of a faith superhero. God promised to reward Abraham abundantly for his simple obedience (see Genesis 12:1–4; Hebrews 11:8).

But if we had been Abraham's friends and neighbors watching his life, we likely would have thought Abraham odd for moving to the desert. We would not have known that a great act of faith was taking place. And if Abraham had explained his move by telling us he was obeying God, we might have thought he had early-onset dementia. We know it was an amazing act of faith only because God tells us. Faith, by its nature, is a matter of the heart, and only God knows the heart.

Most of Abraham's other amazing acts of faith would have appeared unremarkable as well. God told an elderly Abraham that he would father a great nation, even though the hero of faith was past child-bearing age. And when Abraham heard this, he believed God (see Genesis 15:1–6). For that simple act of belief, God accounted it to him as righteousness.

Even if we had been living in Abraham's household at the time, this monumental event would have gone unnoticed. Abraham's tremendous act of faith took place completely within his heart. Perhaps Abraham would have told us what he believed. Even with that, however, we would have no evidence to indicate whether his belief was well-founded or whether he might be delusional. We know in hindsight it was great faith because God reveals to us the heart of Abraham.

Abraham's faith was and is a huge deal. Two thousand years later, Paul highlighted Abraham's story as he inspired his readers with the incredible opportunity *we* have to walk by faith (see Romans 4:1–25). But an impartial onlooker living alongside Abraham would not have known, for faith is something that occurs in heart. And so it usually will be with us. God always knows our heart. He desires to reward greatly those who trust Him. But most of that trust might be invisible to those around us.

None of the major events of Abraham's life involve the sorts of things that fill history books, such as building cities, empires, or river cultures. Ultimately he became the ancestor of a great nation, but his life story can be summarized in one phrase: one man walking by faith in obedience to God. We know of Abraham's greatness only because God tells us Abraham's story.

This leads to a fascinating question: who else is great that God hasn't yet told us about? The answer, amazingly, is that each of us has the opportunity to achieve this sort of greatness. In fact, the Bible exhorts us to follow Abraham's example. But this is a vital perspective to embrace: true greatness often is invisible in our current world.

The World Needs More Superheroes

When I was a boy, my favorite comic superhero was Spider-Man. If you aren't familiar with the story, Peter Parker is a science nerd who gets picked on by athletes and bullies. None of the girls want anything to do with him. One day he's in the science lab conducting an experiment when a radioactive spider bites him. Suddenly he's given all the powers of a spider. He can sense danger even without seeing it; he can lift incredibly heavy objects; he can climb walls. He even invents a spiderweb technology that lets him sling around town.

After Peter begins to exert his new physical strength, his Uncle Ben (with whom he lives) teaches him this very important lesson: "With great power comes great responsibility." Peter doesn't think much of the advice. As he's getting used to his new powers, he sees a robbery in progress. "Not my problem," he tells himself. But sadly his inaction leads to tragedy. The robber kills Peter's Uncle Ben, and Peter lives with a haunted, guilty feeling. He could have stopped a great evil but didn't. He decides to practice Uncle Ben's advice from that point forward.

Peter Parker embraces his social status as a reject in order to protect his true identity as a crime-fighting superhero. So he becomes a superhero who is invisible to his neighbors. Still, embracing his inner superhero doesn't go over well with everyone. The *Daily Bugle,* a fictional newspaper, runs constant smear campaigns against him.

To make the plot even more interesting, Peter works at the newspaper and has to put up with editor Jonah Jameson's contempt for Peter's alter ego.

I watched the cartoons and movies, and I saw the Broadway musical twice. When Terri and I got married, I would get out of bed on Saturday mornings to watch *Spider-Man* cartoons with her. There's something about this story that resonates with me, and—judging from the cultural popularity of the character—with many others. We love it because it points to a greater spiritual truth that we long to live. But it's not just Peter Parker.

The story line of *Spider-Man* echoes the leading themes we see in *Star Wars*, *Harry Potter*, *Lord of the Rings*, *Superman*, *Cinderella*, and *The Chronicles of Narnia*. Think about these stories. Power is channeled into some nerd, underdog, or reject so he or she can fight evil. Usually, however, the protagonist discovers that his or her vast power can't be revealed to the world. So the superhero remains largely invisible to observers and is rejected by the world, even though the nerd is now the agent saving the world.

We all feel like rejects to some degree. This isn't because we don't have a great sense of self or because we need more self-esteem. We feel that way because we are, actually, rejects. For one, the world is fallen from God's original design. Every one of us was created to rule and steward the world in perfect harmony with God and one another, but humanity is clearly falling short of that design. Unlike the alien invaders who are coming to take over the world in the fantasy stories we mentioned, the real world *already* has been taken over by an evil principality. Satan is the real Lex Luthor, the megalomaniac world dictator wannabe from *Superman*. Our job—our superhero mission, if we choose to accept it—is to kick him out of his spot. We accomplish this mission by *living by faith*, just like Abraham. Living by faith might often be invisible in our current age. But if we trust God, adopt the perspective God offers us, and walk in obedience, then we can follow Abraham's example of being a faith superhero.

Yes, you. Yes, me. We've been called to fight an evil superpower in the spiritual world. And a lot of that evil power looks like ordinary selfishness in ordinary activities. We're cloaked, for now, so the world may oppose our actions when we reject selfishness in favor of service. In fact, just as the editor of the *Daily Bugle* rejected Spider-Man, the world also may reject us and even blame us for the world's problems. Even when we fight to hold the world together—Jesus refers to us as salt and light—we might be portrayed as the ones tearing the world apart. This should come as no surprise. Paul told Timothy: "[E]veryone who wants to live a godly life in Christ Jesus will be persecuted" (2 Tim. 3:12).

How to Live Like a Superhero

Abraham is a great example of a biblical superhero because his faith ignited the power to do amazing things in God's economy. And what about us? We have an advantage over Abraham, who lived long before the time of Christ. When we become Christians, we're given the Holy Spirit. And the Spirit living within us is the most potent power in the universe.

You might be tempted to disregard the power of the Holy Spirit. Don't make that mistake. Paul told a group of followers of Jesus that when the Holy Spirit would come upon them, they would receive power (see Acts 1:8). The word *power* in this verse is the Greek word *dunamis,* which is used 120 times in the New Testament. It refers to "strength, power, or ability." We get the English words *dynamite* and *dynamic* from it. Often it refers to miraculous power, as in Mark 5:30 when Jesus felt healing power (*dunamis*) flow out of Him. Clearly the power of God is larger than the power of any comic superhero. But it is spiritual power.

You and I are faced with a serious choice. If you're a Christian, you already have been given the power of the Holy Spirit. The question is whether we will use it. Peter Parker, when he saw the thief, decided not to use his power to stop evil, and he regretted it. That's the same choice each of us has to make each day. And we have to make that choice no matter what state our life is in—whether we find ourselves in the valley, on a mountain top, or on the plains.

Though Peter Parker's aunt and uncle's advice initially sounded to him like an empty platitude, it echoed the words of Christ. Jesus explained, "[E]veryone to whom much was given, of him much will be required" (Luke 12:48). In other words, the greater the gifts that God has given us, the greater our responsibility to help others. At first Peter Parker wanted to use his superhero powers in ways that would solely benefit himself. But he soon realized that fighting evil on behalf of others was the only true way to use his power.

Serving the best interests of others is the life of a Christian and the life of a faith superhero. However, the more superhero-like things we do, the more the world is likely to take advantage of us or even hate us. That's just the way it usually works. When we act in faith, when we acknowledge that we are, in fact, resurrection-empowered creatures, we actually push out the darkness and bring in the Light. The creatures who hang out in the dark don't like it, and they'll strike back.

The underappreciated work of a superhero might look like loving your enemies, turning the other cheek, or letting go of your anxiety no matter how chaotic things become. When we do these things—when we trust and obey God—we ignite the superhero power within us. This sort of faith walk is what the angels are intently studying. Perhaps they are like us when we read a superhero comic or watch a Marvel superhero movie. We watch and are inspired but are not allowed to enter that world.

And sometimes we get to come alongside other like-minded people. And *that* is a real treasure. The award-winning book and film series *Band of Brothers* is wildly popular because it speaks to our very core and shows the unshakeable bonds of love that developed among American GIs during World War II. These bonds could never be forged under ordinary circumstances. They came about only in the awful circumstances of combat. The soldiers didn't want to go to war, but being in the war gave them an extraordinary benefit that could not be gained elsewhere.

This is similar to what's available in our epic adventure. Life, even on the most routine day, is a never-to-be-repeated opportunity to experience a bond born of trust. Just as soldiers develop bonds during war, Scripture tells us that we are at war with some of the same principalities and powers today. As we saw in Job, Satan and his followers want us to fail, while the angels study us in order to know God. When we battle in a way that shows our trust in God, we come to see God as Job saw God.

In ways we don't fully understand, we make an enormous impact on the unseen world. And often there is an immediate benefit. I have experienced a bond of "brotherhood" established from standing alongside fellow believers in the war against unseen forces. The bond is forged when we go into battle by faith. These are among the greatest rewards we can experience this side of heaven. But they come through difficulties, even difficulties that might seem quite ordinary to outside observers.

It can be difficult to remember that our true battle is in the spiritual realm. But by faith, we know it to be true. Faith is, by definition, something we believe but do not see. The apostle Paul reminded the believers living at Ephesus of this unseen spiritual battle. He told them to put on spiritual armor each day, much like a Roman centurion would dress for battle. "For we do not wrestle against flesh and blood, but against principalities, against powers, against the rulers of the darkness of this age, against spiritual hosts of wickedness in the heavenly places" (Eph. 6:12).

We aren't called to merely cope with the evil of this world. We're called to fight it and to overcome it, secure in the knowledge that the battle already has been won. As weird as it may sound, I now feel loved by God because He asks me to do hard things.

Are we only to pray, or does spiritual warfare include open conflict in the physical world? As history shows, it's both. William Wilberforce, for example, tenaciously waged a savvy, lifelong political battle in England to eliminate the slave trade. He believed God was calling him to that fight. To win he had to stand against powerful business interests and the attendant cronyism that always infects politics and government.

Similarly, when you take a stance, people may not like it. It is likely that as you strive to speak the truth, people will react negatively to hearing something they don't want to hear. The truer it is, the more negatively they will react. Jesus didn't sugarcoat his criticism of the Pharisees, and they didn't take kindly to it. In fact, they plotted to kill him. He told them the truth anyway.

Unless I actively seek what is good for others, relying on guidance from the Holy Spirit, I naturally will default to serving myself. But we have the power to seek good for other people, as unto the Lord, when we activate it by faith. Just like a Roman soldier had to put on his armor each day, so we must daily arm ourselves with truth and faith. We're promised in 1 John 4:4: "[T]he One who is in you is greater than the one who is in the world." Let's go out there and act like it.

We all may be rejected by a fallen world; however, that does not diminish the reality that we have been chosen for a high purpose, the *highest* purpose. You are a faith Spider-Man, Wonder Woman, or Superman. Christians must harness the power of a true perspective because they are charged with bringing restoration to a corrupted Earth.

Unless we choose a true perspective about who we are and why God has placed us here, we may miss this incredible opportunity. Will we fail along the way? Of course. I fail all the time. The superhero stories are interesting because the heroes struggle with difficulty and failure. But there is a reason God begins each day with a brand-new dawn. Walking by faith is a daily challenge for every one of us. Fortunately, God offers us a daily provision of grace and mercy—a fresh start for a superhero day.

8

HARNESSING YOUR TRUE PERSPECTIVE

As we have seen, a number of false perspectives compete for our loyalty. We can believe the lie that it's possible to control your everyday circumstances. We can believe that if we avoid God we also can avoid the tests that God's children face. We can believe in the power of our intellect, our resourcefulness, and our earthly wisdom.

Or we can identify the lies inherent in every false perspective and choose instead to follow God by adopting and living according to the true perspective He offers. I like to say that life is a team sport. And often a true perspective is something we need help to find.

On September 22, 2015, I went to the church for a rehearsal of Moriah's memorial service, my heart full of grief and sorrow. I sat in an empty pew as my children practiced the service. Our son David isn't the only musical member of our family. David, our son Wally, and our daughter Becky all took the stage to sing, while our daughter-in-law Lindsy (Luke's wife) played the piano. They sang four songs: David's "Today Is Beautiful" and the worship songs "You're Beautiful," "Good, Good Father," and "Waiting for Love."

I listened as the kids went through the program, the warmth of their music like a soothing hug for my soul.

"I've seen many searching for answers far and wide, but I know we're all searching for answers only you provide," they sang. "'Cause you know just what we need before we say a word. You're a good, good Father." It was a reminder that the circumstance of Moriah's death really, really stinks, but I know God still has our best interests at heart. I think, somehow, it was more the music than the words that provided such relief. Music is a language that can't be translated; God was speaking comfort through the notes. They ministered to me in a way that pierced me to the core. There was nothing comfortable about that circumstance, but God was being my comfort, letting me know He was still with me.

God wants us to live *above* the circumstances of life. I wish I could tell you that it's easy to harness a true perspective and live a faith-walk that looks above the circumstances to see God at work. I would never tell you that. Instead, I'm living proof that living above the circumstances is a daily struggle. I mess up a lot. But the great, invigorating news is that each day brings a fresh opportunity to be a superhero in God's economy. Simply by being faithful throughout the various terrains of life, including (and especially) the very mundane, everyday tasks and interactions, we live a faith superhero life.

David and Mary Kathryn collaborated to write the title song for David's album *Yellow Balloons,* which commemorates and serves as a memorial to Moriah. It expresses the honest reality that we can't make sense of why God would allow this, but that means we need God's help even more.

It recognizes the reality that pain and grief will be with us for a long time, probably the rest of our lives. But that also means we need God even more.

David told me he gets a couple of messages each week from people who have lost a child and were ministered to by this song. Here are some of the lyrics:

> God, what were you doing?
> What were you doing here?
> I know that you are moving
> But right now, it's less than clear.
> 'Cause the world just got darker
> 'Cause a little light went out the
> And we'll try to hold it together
> But it's hard to do that now.
>
> So we'll cry on her birthdays
> As days turn to years
> We beg for your wisdom
> Can't go on without you near
> 'Cause our beautiful girl
> Left the world
> Left the world.[21]

Are you going through agonizing challenges? Remember, God is good even now. It is okay to search, to wonder, to ask. Don't despair in the valley. God's best is not always to give us comfortable circumstances, but it always is for Him to be our comfort.

Are you living life and feeling bored by the tedium? Remember that God loves you and that remaining faithful in the seemingly ordinary things of life is heroic. Don't get demoralized by the plains.

Are you wealthier than you've ever been? Remember we're just stewards. Don't cling to the mountaintops, just keep following the One who took you there in the first place.

Choosing a true perspective allows you to be a faith superhero who looks above the circumstances rather than being crushed underneath them. We're here to learn to know God by faith—a privilege even angels don't have. We're here to shut up Satan, even though we are new arrivals, infants in comparison to angelic beings. And somehow we play a part in God's work of restoring the earth. As the Christian author J.R.R. Tolkien's character Gandalf says in the movie *The Hobbit*, "Some believe it is only great power that can hold evil in check, but that is not what I have found. It is the small everyday deeds of ordinary folk that keep the darkness at bay. Small acts of kindness and love."[22] Living faithfully even in small things holds the world together in some mystical way. We are here to learn to rule the earth in loving service, rather than as tyrants.

The opportunity to know God by faith is a rare, once-in-an-existence opportunity, and it takes on a different look depending on which type of circumstance you're in. Circumstances, remember, are just our opportunity to learn. No matter where you find yourself today, you can choose a true perspective. Don't waste another second by believing the lies of the world.

Only by harnessing a true perspective can you truly make the most of your brief life on Earth.

Buckle up.

If you want more resources to help you live a faithful life of service, visit www.trueservantleadership.com/.

DISCUSSION GUIDE

This guide is designed to help you get the most from reading *Yellow Balloons*. You can use this discussion guide on your own as you ask God to reveal His truth and to work in your life. No matter where you are personally—living on a mountaintop, in a valley, or on the plains—these questions will help you explore biblical themes to see more clearly how they apply to your life.

You also can use the guide in talking with a friend over coffee. Discuss the questions, chapter by chapter, as the two of you read through the book. Likewise, these questions are useful in a small-group setting. You can listen to a song from David Dunn that corresponds with each chapter. These songs can be found at the iTunes store or on YouTube. Discussing *Yellow Balloons* together can help you and members of your group learn how to live faithfully in any circumstance of life.

Chapter 1: That Day

Listen to "Yellow Balloons"
https://www.youtube.com/watch?v=5Btot3TeM2k

1. Author Tim Dunn lost his granddaughter Moriah when she was just twenty-two months old. After describing the gut-wrenching day when Moriah died, Dunn ends Chapter 1 by writing that members of his family had to decide which perspective each person would choose.

    • What perspective did his family choose about grieving, and what impact did it make?
    • What are some of the perspectives we can choose in such a situation?

2. Note that the author immediately began seeking advice after Moriah's death. He was looking for a proper perspective.

    • Why do we need help from others to gain a proper perspective when we encounter difficulty?

- How can we gain great advantage by seeking a correct perspective when hard things occur?

3. Have you considered that choosing a perspective on the circumstances you face has a great bearing on what you do, including living faithfully as a child of God?

   - If so, how has that affected the way you live out your faith?
   - If not, how can you deliberately seek the best perspective to change how you deal with circumstances in the future?

4. Moriah's pediatrician kindly reassured her parents that there was nothing they could have done to prevent her death. But there are times when one or more persons are responsible for tragedy.

   - How would that influence the perspective you choose?
   - When we are the cause of the problem, what are some additional steps we need to take?

Chapter 2: The Angels Are Watching

Listen to "Psalm 8"
https://www.youtube.com/watch?v=15O-KJURXec

1. The primary point that drives *Yellow Balloons* is an observation that we can control only three things: whom we trust, what we do, and the perspective we choose in any situation.

   - How does our chosen perspective affect whom we trust and what we do?
   - If we have an untrue perspective about God, how does that affect our ability to trust God?
   - If we have a true perspective, how does that affect our ability to make good choices?

2. List things we often try to control that are not within our control.

   - Why do we try so hard to control what is uncontrollable?

- What does this tendency say about the perspective we choose when we try to control other people or future events, which are beyond our control?

3. Think about what is causing you anxiety? Is it related to your trying to control something or someone?
   - How might a change in perspective help you in this area?
   - Discuss how freeing it can be when you realize that each person makes his or her own choices.

4. In Chapter 2, the author writes that we tend to live "under the circumstances" as victims of our wrong perspectives. A victim is someone who does not have a choice.
   - What perspectives cause us to be imprisoned by our circumstances, to live as though we have no choices?
   - Do you find this in your life? If so, what perspective can you choose that will set you free?

5. A pastor counseled the author to "embrace" grief by grieving with others when and how they want to grieve. He said you will hurt more but heal faster. And you will grow closer. The author decided that perspective was true and a worthwhile investment in others.

    - Do you think this makes sense? What might embracing grief look like for you?
    - How could that help, even in circumstances less tragic than the loss of a child?

6. We learn from reading Ephesians 3:10 and 1 Peter 1:12 that angels watch *us* and learn *from us* about the things of God.

    - How does it affect you to know angels watch your life to learn about God? Is there an area in which you are inspired to change or to exercise more faith?
    - What do you think of the perspective that our lives on Earth are a once-in-

an-existence opportunity to know God by faith?

- What are the practical outcomes of believing that learning to know God by faith is the true path to ultimate fulfillment?

Chapter 3: Perspective in the Valley

Listen to "Grace Will Lead Me Home"
https://www.youtube.com/watch?v=O3WeqqTKqhU

1. Getting a grip on unvarnished reality is the first step in adopting a true perspective. We must see life as it truly is. And as the author learned from admitting his faults, this can be excruciating.

- Did you find it surprising that he identified with the scene from *The Chronicles of Narnia* in which Aslan removes a dragon skin from the bratty boy Eustace? How do you sense that deep pain ultimately benefitted Tim Dunn?

- The author said this experience set him free from a faulty image of himself. How can having a wrong perspective about yourself enslave you?
- Recall a personal experience—which ultimately benefitted you—in which you came to grips with a painful reality.

2. Job responded to his severe trial with an amazing view of God. "I will gratefully accept whatever God brings me; it is His prerogative. He gave me life in the first place, and all I have came from Him. If He wants it back, it is His to take." This was not at all what Satan had predicted. This statement about God was Job's worship, and afterward God rubbed Satan's nose in Job's righteousness.

- What can we learn from Job about choosing a proper perspective about God?
- Does it surprise you that someone could already be this righteous and,

even then, God still wants him to have more?

- What does that tell you about God and what He desires for us?

3. The author makes it clear that God always has our best interest at heart. He wants so much more good for us than a transaction with a manipulatable god could provide. At times we treat God like a cosmic vending machine. We decide what we need and pull a lever trying to get God to supply our need.

- Why do we do this? Do you feel it's an attempt to control God? Why or why not?
- Job's friends and Satan all claimed that God was like a cosmic vending machine, which angered God. Do you believe God really does have our best interest at heart in every instance? How will your perspective be shaped by how you answer that question?

4. We read in 1 Corinthians 10:13 that God only allows temptations into our lives that we can bear. That means God decides which circumstances we are allowed to encounter.

   • Do you find comfort in God's taking ultimate responsibility for what happened to Job at the time He gave Satan permission to attack Job? Why or why not?

   • How can this reality affect our ability to embrace every circumstance as a gift and an opportunity?

   • Do you find it surprising that knowing God by faith turns out to be an eternal treasure worth an immense amount of difficulty? How will embracing that perspective affect the way you live?

5. Job came to see God not just as a power who does as He pleases, but also as the One who sees all things truly. Job came to know that God's perspective is unlimited and true, which deepened the intimacy

in Job's relationship with God. How does our view of God affect the intimacy of our relationship with Him?

- Consider ways you can view God more accurately and how that can lead to a deeper relationship with Him.

Chapter 4: Perspective on the Plains

Listen to "Kingdom"

https://www.youtube.com/watch?v=6nfo8xOwlK8

1. Most of our lives are spent on the "plains," that is in the seemingly ordinary routines of life. But the Bible teaches that ordinary or small things are actually big things (see Colossians 3:23–24). Have you been seduced into thinking that you have to do amazing things for God in order to live a successful spiritual life?

   - What does a Colossians 3:23 perspective that God greatly values us doing routine things well mean to your everyday life? How does it affect your routine tasks when you adopt the perspective that God is watching and desires to reward you greatly when you complete those tasks "heartily" in order to please God?

- How does this perspective affect the choices you make at home and at work?

2. Our heavenly Father is always willing to spend special moments with us, similar to the author's time on the "trampene" with his granddaughter Moriah. Jesus tells us in Revelation 3:19–21 that He is always outside the door of our heart, desiring to commune with us. He uses the image of dining together, one of the most intimate ways to commune.

- Is this a new perspective to you on how God sees you? Do you believe He *likes* you and wants to be with you?
- Revelation 3:19 says Jesus also will discipline us when we need it. Are you capable of viewing God as the ideal

Father? Do any negative experiences you have had with your earthly father prevent you from seeing God in this way? If so, what are steps you can take to begin to see God the Father as One who desires the best for you?

3. The author presents being in the family of God as a free gift without condition that we receive simply by believing.

   - How do we benefit from adopting a perspective that we are God's children and He will love us and wants the best for us no matter what we do? (For further study on the free "gift" of life see John 3:16; Ephesians 2:8–9; John 10:28.)

4. The author also writes that although spiritual birth is an unconditional gift received by faith, gaining the full benefit of this gift depends on the choices we make. The author points to Colossians 3:23–24, which says, "And whatever you

do, do it heartily, as to the Lord and not to men, knowing that from the Lord you will receive the reward of the inheritance . . ."

- How does it benefit us to adopt the perspective that the rewards of life, and a rewarding life, very much depend on whether we walk in obedience to Jesus' commands? (For further study on the "prize" of life see 2 Corinthians 5:10; Matthew 6:20–21; Revelation 22:12.)

- How does this perspective bring about a change in how we view life's opportunities? How does it cause us to view the choices we make? How does it affect how we view striving and what we ought to strive for?

5. Brother Lawrence wrote: "We ought not grow weary of doing little things for the love of God, who regards not the greatness of the work, but the love with which it is performed." Brother Lawrence became famous because he did routine kitchen

tasks as "unto the Lord." Helen Keller admitted, "I long to accomplish a great and noble task, but it is my chief duty to accomplish small tasks as if they were great and noble."

- Reflect on the major roles you fill (spouse, parent, friend, neighbor, community member, boss, or employee) and how those roles are affected when we practice this perspective. If this is new to you, try practicing Brother Lawrence's approach of communing with God at the same time you perform a routine task. Think of it in the same way as having a meal with Him.

- What is the potential advantage of living with the constant awareness that God is in us and with us, and we can commune with Him constantly, even as we do "small" things?

6. The Bible takes this thinking one step further. Not only does it matter how we

perform small things, but in fact, small things are big things. We see these truths in the story of the widow's mite and the promise of eternal rewards for doing "small" things such as providing a cup of cold water or performing day-to-day tasks with excellence. The author presents doing these small things, such as giving cups of cool water in Jesus' name, as the path to winning a great victory, like a Greek Olympic medal (1 Cor. 9:24–27).

- We all care what others think of us. Take a few moments to reflect on how much you really care about what Jesus thinks about your life.
- Do you think it's worth striving for praise from Jesus for the small deeds you do for others?
- What impacts would you anticipate when you apply this perspective on a daily basis?

7. How does adopting the perspective that all our money is God's affect how we view

money? Have you ever struggled with being stingy toward others but generous when you spend money on yourself? The parable of the unrighteousness steward (Luke 16:1–16) teaches us that God wants us to be shrewd in using His resources (which He entrusted to us) to benefit others. It teaches us that when we do this, we create a huge benefit for ourselves in the next life.

- Do you believe this? How does that perspective affect how you deal with money?

8. Is there an area of your life in which you feel particularly weary? How can the truths of Chapter 4 help you persevere and even thrive?

9. One principle for thriving and finding joy on the plains is to remember you are judged by what you do with what has been entrusted to you, not by what you would do with what you don't have.

Another principle is that second steps can only follow first steps.

- Is there an area of your life where you could stop waiting on something and start acting in faith with what you already have? What area comes to mind? Is there a first step you can take?

Chapter 5: Perspective on the Mountaintop

Listen to "Today is Beautiful and Ready to Be Myself"

https://www.youtube.com/watch?v=hFLgmvzk-ik

https://www.youtube.com/watch?v=nfOZ_r5YuS0

1. What is the world's perspective on "mountaintop" experiences (riches, prestige, fame, success, showing the world that you have "arrived")? The Bible says God has given us richly all things to enjoy (1 Tim. 6:17). In addition, Dunn interprets the parable of the rich young ruler to mean we should consider everything we have to be God's and live as a steward or manager.

- How do you balance not trusting in "uncertain riches" with "enjoying all things God has richly given us" (1 Tim. 6:17)?
- What do you think about "deeding" everything over to God in recognition that everything we have is His and is just passing through our hands on its way to somewhere else?
- What are some practical steps we can take to "deed over" to God, the rightful owner of all things?

2. Jesus' disciples reached the mountaintop because Jesus led them there. Peter's idea was to build some huts and stay there.

- How can clinging to a mountaintop experience cause us to lose track of following Jesus?

3. After the mountaintop experience, Jesus led the disciples back into the valley to serve others.

- What are some things we can do to help us follow Jesus back down from mountaintops and keep our eyes on following Him?

4. Which physical possessions bring you joy? Which physical possessions mainly bring you trouble?

- What do you think of the author's advice to get rid of physical possessions that we don't enjoy?
- Are you generous with your finances? How can generosity lead to financial freedom?
- Are there any possessions or funds that own *you* rather than you owning them?

5. Reflect on the world's materialistic definition of happiness. If you understand happiness to be "getting something you don't have" there will be no lasting happiness as a result. Instead, you will need something else you don't have.

- Do you find enjoyment in what you already have, or do you believe happiness depends on acquiring something else?
- How can adopting the perspective that God has given you circumstances that are just what you need lead you to greater happiness?

6. How much are you driven by what other people think of you? The reality is that we never truly know what others think of us. The fact is that they probably are not thinking about us, but rather wondering what we think about them. Jesus told us what we can do so that He will think well of us.

   - Do you believe that when we obey Jesus it makes Him pleased with us?
   - How can we find freedom in trusting that Jesus is pleased when we follow Him?

7.   The Bible tells us we can buy gold from God by listening to Him. What are some practical ways to listen to God?

8.   A mountaintop experience can be one of our greatest trials. It temps us to believe we can do it ourselves instead of walking by faith as we depend on the Spirit. It's easy to start relying on our own "smarts" and think we know better than God. Or we can rely on spiritual experiences rather than relying on God.

   • What are some strategies you can adopt to keep from falling into this trap?
   • The truth is that our intellects are tiny in comparison to God's, no matter the level of our IQ. Our experiences should inform us, not define us. What are the practical benefits of living with this perspective?

9.   Of the four kinds of prosperity discussed in Chapter 5 (riches, prestige, intelligence, and spiritual highs), which

poses the greatest danger for you? What is the true perspective on these gifts?

Chapter 6: What Is a Job-Like Experience?

Listen to "Wanna Go Back"
https://www.youtube.com/watch?v=yUvxhGRUR3s

1. The author defines a Job-like experience as any experience that brings intense pain. Take a moment to list the Job-like experiences over the course of your life.

   • Has your perspective on these experiences changed over time?
   • What perspective do you have about the experiences now?

2. Tim Dunn suggests that it's all right—and even modeled by Jesus—to ask God to deliver you from Job-like experiences. But ultimately, regardless of God's answer, the right and true perspective is "I know that you [God] know best and that you love

me perfectly. I know you want the best for me, so I will embrace whatever you give me."

- In what way(s) can you start to practice this?
- How can adopting this perspective bring peace and happiness?

3. "Our experiences . . . give us the chance to become all God meant us to be. Separation is painful, but love is forever. It is all a matter of perspective . . ." What do these words from Chapter 6 mean to you?

4. The author writes: "Learning to choose a true perspective has immense practical application in *any* situation." If your Job-like experiences have never made sense to you, how might pursuing a true perspective help you?

5. C. S. Lewis wrote, "It would seem that our Lord finds our desires not too strong, but too weak. We are half-hearted creatures,

fooling around with drink and sex and ambition when infinite joy is offered to us, like an ignorant child who wants to go on making mud pies in a slum because he cannot imagine what is meant by the offer of a holiday at sea."[23]

- In what areas are you settling for mud pies in a slum?
- How can you change your perspective to seek God's best for your life?

Chapter 7: Embrace Your Inner Superhero

Listen to "History"

https://www.youtube.com/watch?v=7thehGvWoJ4

1. What is your favorite superhero, princess tale or adventure story? What is it about the hero that appeals to you, that you identify with?

   - What are some ways you can be like that hero in the realm of your faith-walk?

- Do you really believe that you have amazing inner power that you can unleash by faith?

2. The Bible tells us that Abraham's faith was amazing. It made him a faith superhero. But the author points out that if we had lived alongside Abraham, we likely would not have known, because faith is largely a matter of the heart. The actions Abraham took would not necessarily have convinced us he had great faith.

    - How does this encourage you? Do you believe that following God in small ways can be living a superhero-status life?
    - How will adopting this perspective affect the choices you make on a daily basis?

3. Are there ways in which you feel rejected? Does it encourage you that the world's rejection of those who live out their faith is

in fact an aspect of living a faith superhero life?

- If we adopt the perspective of being a faith superhero, how does that affect all the "little" things we do each day?
- How can this perspective meld with Brother Lawrence's perspective about doing kitchen tasks to please God and in fellowship with God?

4. The author writes that although we are "small" (as we learned in Job's story), we are faith superheroes when we walk daily with a seed of faith and the indwelling power of the Holy Spirit.

- How does the admission of being "small" lead to walking in dependence on Jesus and serving others as a faith superhero?

5. The world sees Peter Parker (Spider-Man) as a nerdy kid who works at a newspaper. But in reality he is a superhero making the world a better place. The author reminds

us that sometimes being a faith superhero might look like simply loving your enemies, turning the other cheek, or not being anxious and giving thanks in all things.

- Would your perspective on life change if you approached all its terrains, even the mundane life on the plains, from the vantage point of being a faith superhero?
- What are some tangible steps you can take along this path?

6. Do you believe that God's Spirit indwells you and that the Spirit provides the superhero *dunamis* or dynamite power? What sorts of things do you have the supernatural power to accomplish through the Spirit?

- What type of actions does the Bible define as faith-superhero types of actions?
- What is one change you can make because you have adopted this perspective?

7. Whether we live as faith superheroes is a matter of choice—what we decide to do with the great responsibility we have been given.

- What are the things in your world worth fighting for?
- What things are worth the struggle and the inevitable rejection involved in being a faith superhero?
- Which fears might prevent you from coming along on the adventure God is offering? Or from acting courageously in some arena where He is calling you?
- What are some faith-superhero assignments God is calling you to?

Chapter 8: Harnessing Your True Perspective

Listen to "Masterpiece"

https://www.youtube.com/watch?v=Opzf_RdT0TA

1. The author writes: "God wants us to live *over the circumstances* of life."

- What are some circumstances you might be living "under"?
- What perspective do you need to adopt that might turn a circumstance from a limitation into an opportunity?

2. One of the three things we control as humans is the perspective we decide take about our life experiences.

- What perspective do you have that might not be true? About yourself? About others? About God? About your possessions? About your importance? About your opportunity to do amazing things?

3. Which "terrain" of life is currently the most challenging for you—the mountaintop, the valley, or the plains? Why? What true perspective should you adopt about that terrain?

4. Which shift in perspective can help you have less anxiety, freeing you to experience

more purpose and helping you thrive in that terrain?

5. Getting to know God by faith is a rare, once-in-an-existence opportunity, one that fascinates even the angels. How can you grow your faith and know Him better during the time you have?

6. Think about today. How were you given the chance to be a faith superhero, according to the author's definition? Did you seize it?

7. The author wants you to know that writing this book brought the pain of grief every time he worked on it. As he wrote he relived losing Moriah, but he thought it was worth it to make an investment in you. He believes you are worth it, even though he might never meet you in this life.

   • Is there anything in your life you have been reluctant to share that could bless others?

- Will you consider being "shrewd" and investing in others by sharing your grief, your faults, and the lessons you have learned?

ENDNOTES

1. Jacob Merrill Manning, *Sermons and Addresses* (Boston: Houghton, Mifflin, 1889), 521.

2. Guy Winch, "Why Rejection Hurts so Much— and What to Do about It" (TED Talk at TEDxLinnaeusUniveristy, Växjö, Kronobergs län, Sweden, November 7, 2014).

3. Philip Yancey, *Where is God When It Hurts?* (Grand Rapids: Zondervan, 1977), 108.

4. C.S. Lewis, *The Voyager of the Dawn Treader* (New York : Macmillan, 1952).

5. Oswald Chambers, "Impulsiveness or Discipleship?" My Utmost for His Highest, accessed April 23, 2018. https://utmost.org/impulsiveness-or-discipleship/.

6. Dorothy Sayers, "Why Work?" in *Creed or Chaos* (New York: Harcourt Brace, 1949). Retrieved from http://centerforfaithandwork.com/article/why-work-dorothy-sayers.

7. Ibid.

8. Mark A. Powell, *Giving to God* (Grand Rapids: Eerdmans, 2006), 85.

9. A.P. Fitt, W.R. Moody and A. McConnell, *Record of a Christian Work* (East Northfield: Record of a Christian Work Co., 1881).

10. Helen Keller, The Quotations Page, accessed April 23, 2018. http://www.quotationspage.com/quote/41473.html.

11. Harold J. Chadwick, quoted in *The Practice of the Presence of God* by Brother Lawrence (Alachua: Bridge-Logos, 1999), 90-91.

12. Martin Luther King Jr., "What Is Your Life's Blueprint?" (speech at Barratt Junior High School, Philadelphia, PA, October 26, 1967), accessed April 23, 2018. http://old.seattletimes.com/special/mlk/king/blueprint.html.

13. David Dunn, "Today Is Beautiful," released June 2015, track 3 on *Crystal Clear*, BEC Recordings. compact disc.

14. Carrey, Jim. Twitter post. September 10, 2017, 6:24 PM. Retrieved from https://twitter.com/officialcarrey/status/907052189448843264?lang=en

15. William James, Dictionary of Quotes, accessed April 23, 2018. https://www.dictionary-quotes.

com/the-greatest-use- of-life- is-to- spend-it- for-something- that-will- outlast-it- william-james/.

16. David Dunn, "Today Is Beautiful," released June 2015, track 6 on *Crystal Clear*, BEC Recordings. compact disc.

17. John Calvin, Calvin Quotes, accessed April 23, 2018. http://calvinquotes.com/self-confidence/.

18. Quoted by Hans K. LaRondelle, "Luther and the gospel," *Ministry Magazine*, accessed April 23, 2018. https://www.ministrymagazine.org/archive/2000/11/luther-and-the-gospel.

19. Oswald Chambers, *My Utmost for His Highest* (London: Marshall, Morgan, & Scott, 1927).

20. Quoted by David Mathis, "We Are Far Too Easily Pleased," Desiring God, accessed April 23, 2018. https://www.desiringgod.org/articles/we-are-far-too-easily-pleased.

21. David Dunn, "Yellow Balloons," released February 2017, track 10 on *Yellow Balloons*, BEC Recordings. compact disc.

22. *The Hobbit: An Unexpected Journey,* directed by Peter Jackson (2012; Burbank, CA: Warner Brothers, 2013), DVD.